To renew this book, phone 0845 1202811 or visit
our website at www.libcat.oxfordshire.gov.uk
You will need your library PIN number
(available from your library)

OXFORDSHIRE
COUNTY COUNCIL
SOCIAL & COMMUNITY SERVICES
www.oxfordshire.gov.uk

3303605355

THE ARCHITECTURE AND LEGACY OF BRITISH RAILWAY BUILDINGS

1825 TO PRESENT DAY

ROBERT THORNTON AND MALCOLM WOOD

THE ARCHITECTURE AND LEGACY OF BRITISH RAILWAY BUILDINGS

1825 TO PRESENT DAY

ROBERT THORNTON AND MALCOLM WOOD

THE CROWOOD PRESS

First published in 2020 by
The Crowood Press Ltd
Ramsbury, Marlborough
Wiltshire SN8 2HR

www.crowood.com
enquiries@crowood.com

British Library Cataloguing-in-Publication Data
A catalogue record for this book is available from the British Library.

ISBN 978 1 78500 711 8

Frontispiece: Blackfriars Station. (Drawing: Robert Thornton)
Cover images
Front cover: Paul Childs (St Pancras)
Back cover upper photographs, clockwise from top left: Paul Childs (Margate station);
Robert Thornton (Birmingham New Street signal box); Network Rail Archive (Margate Station);
Robert Thornton (Leeds wagon hoist); Malcolm Wood (Stoke on Trent station);
Robert Thornton (Norwich Thorpe station)
Back cover lower photograph: Paul Childs (London Bridge)
Inside back flap upper photograph: Robert Thornton (Midland Hotel Morecambe)
Inside back flap lower photograph: Paul Childs (Glasgow Central station)

Typeset by Derek Doyle & Associates, Shaw Heath
Printed and bound in India by Parksons Graphics

Contents

MANY PEOPLE HAVE BEEN CONSULTED and have helped in the development of this book. We should particularly like to thank Andy Savage and Paul Childs at the Railway Heritage Trust for the assistance with many of the photographs contained within it.

We are indebted to Network Rail for advice and assistance from Vicky Stretch; Trevor Dawton; Gillian Booker; Donna Mitchell; Tom Higginson; Anthony Dewar; Frank Anatole; Trevor Wilson; Ali Al-Said; and Isabelle Milford.

We have appreciated assistance and, indeed, offers of assistance from friends and former colleagues and although, in some cases, memories of events and specific projects are fading, they have nonetheless provided valuable insight into the life and times of railway architectural practice over the second half of the twentieth century and up to the present day. In this context, and in no particular order, we should like to acknowledge assistance provided by John Kitcher; Lis Ager-Harris; Alastair Lansley; Richard Golding; Julian Wormleighton; Bob Yorke; Clive Brandon; Richard Horne; Mike Soden; Barry Gray; Tony Howard; Frances and Michael Edwards; Tony Pike; Andy Parrett; John Fellows; John Ives; Roger and Holly Tillot; Peter Ledhill; Steve Warbis; John Evans; Ian Jamieson; Rob Hayward; Martyn Cornwall; John Stonor; Gordon Williams; Bert Morris; Bruce Methven; Peter Trewin; Jon Cunningham and Jerry Martin. Thank you also to Dave Harris, Coordinator, Midland Rail Study Centre; Francis Thomas at West Midlands Trains Ltd and Julie Okpa at the Department for Transport.

Particular mention should be made of former colleague, Lawrence Jackman, who passed away in 2014 and we should like to thank Lawrence's son, Richard, for permission and assistance to reproduce his father's original perspective drawings, some of which have not been seen since they were produced nearly sixty years ago.

A number of consultant architects involved with the works described in the book have also assisted with information, drawings or photographs and our particular thanks go to John McAslan (John McAslan and Partners); Adam Brown (Landholt and Brown); Mark Middleton (Grimshaw Global); Rob Naybour (Weston Williamson and Partners); Gary Seed (Seed Architects); Peter Jenkins (Building Design Partnership Ltd, Manchester); Tony Howard (Transport Design Consultancy); and Henry Lambon and Wallace Henning (Henning Ltd).

Note: Permission to use the British Rail corporate ID images in Chapter 10 is granted by the Secretary of State for Transport.

And finally, we would both like to thank our wives, Terry and Kuka, and our families for their patience and understanding (!), particularly during all those periods when we appeared to be concentrating on something else and putting off those essential tasks.

THE HISTORY OF RAILWAY BUILDINGS AND the unique architectural idiom that relates to them is nearly two hundred years old and whilst there may be some low spots amongst the highlights, the story continues to be a fascinating one representing all manner of social, commercial, technological and design developments.

The architecture supporting railway operations in the current era has room for all design approaches whether this be in respect of new build, adaptation or full-on restoration. There is also, valuably, room for imaginative reinterpretation and, indeed, a combination of all three. This is a long way from the mono-directional approach of former railway eras and this book pinpoints when this change occurs.

Good and lasting railway architecture doesn't happen on its own. It needs enthusiastic architects, engineers, project managers and, above all, 'clients' who share the same passion in an industry that continues to evolve. It is hoped that the examples and themes illustrated in this book help to stimulate interest and care in both the historic and current railway buildings' portfolios.

IF ONE WERE TO STAND IN A NEWLY MODERNIZED or refurbished station now amidst a thronging mass of commuters and had no knowledge of its history, it might be a surprise to know that one is playing a part in a transport system that is very nearly two hundred years old. Unlike many operational or industrial buildings of this vintage, it is still being used for its original purpose.

Railway architecture is one of the most interesting branches of the bigger subject matter encapsulating and expressing all manner of cultural, commercial and technological influences whilst being simultaneously driven by the unique functional requirements and imperatives of railway operations.

The railway building portfolio has comprised, at each stage in its history, many building types, large and small and of all architectural qualities. Whilst stations may be the most familiar buildings, these represent only a small part of a vast collection of buildings that made up the railway estate until well into the 1960s when cuts to the system in the face of the growth in road transport started to take hold.

The advent of the railways brought with it many new building types such as stations, signal boxes, locomotive 'roundhouses', grand tunnel portals, water towers and the plethora of less well-recorded buildings that supported the new system. Whilst many of these no longer exist, there remains a large and diverse range of railway buildings still evident and in use, even if not for railway purposes. These, together with many other buildings and structures such as bridges, tunnels and viaducts, make up a very rich and diverse catalogue of architectural forms that have contributed so much to the history of Great Britain since the reign of George IV.

Railway architecture across its many functions and applications is a genre that is generally well recognized as unique in this country and appears wherever railway systems spread their influence around the

A true monument to the early years of railway operations, the wagon hoist designed by Sir John Hawkshaw in 1854 was one of a pair standing either side of the viaduct running through Leeds station. Once standing forlorn, it now commands a central position in the developing business district off Wellington Street. (Photo: Robert Thornton)

world. Without the functional drivers inherent in the conveyance of passengers and goods from one part of the country to the next on a track-based system, there would be no railway architecture as such.

Two principal factors lie at the heart of the physical character of today's railway infrastructure. The first is the nature of rail operations and the need for specialist buildings to support these, sometimes unique operational needs, for example, signal boxes and stations. The second is the constraint imposed by the topography and geography of the British Isles on the requirement for a level, or as near-level track as possible.

The combination of these has conspired to produce a new idiom in the architectural canon from the advent of the first railways and which, many years later, still informs the railway buildings of today. The architecture thus produced can be joyous, monumental, awe-inspiring and endlessly fascinating, whether it is liked or reviled: it is certainly distinctive and, in many cases, unique.

The inherited legacy of the railway system, which provides many physical constraints upon infrastructure development, provides a continual challenge that all railway managers, operators, infrastructure designers and construction specialists face every day. It is important to stress that, whilst the railway system that exists today is built on these historic foundations, it is very much a live and current transport network playing a vital and essential role in the continually changing economic and cultural well-being of this country. As such, it has needed to adapt continuously to meet contemporary and predicted needs – the latter, for investment planning purposes usually being twenty-five to thirty years into the future.

The path of progress between what can be recognized as the beginnings of the system and today's railway has not been straightforward, seeing both evolutionary and sometimes rapid growth and, in the instance of the major pruning of the system in the mid-1960s, revolutionary change.

The Book

As a subject of interest to a great many people there are, of course, many books written about aspects of railway architecture. However, those in general circulation tend to focus on passenger stations, mainly of the Victorian and Edwardian eras with only a relatively small number of references to those built in the periods since. However, the more recent flagship developments at stations such as King's Cross and St Pancras in London, which combine contemporary architecture with historic settings, are now receiving greater attention. It is therefore hoped that this book can fill in a few gaps regarding a wider range of buildings and of later periods, particularly the time following the major railway system reorganizations of the second half of the twentieth century.

This book is not intended to be a critical discourse on individual pieces of railway architecture but aspires to tell the story of the practical and architectural ambitions of the wide variety of railway companies when serving the many functional needs of the industry and its customers. There is not enough room in a book such as this to do justice to the scale and variety of the architecture making up the railway portfolio as it stands today, from the humble plate-layers hut to the grandest terminal, but it is hoped that by looking at the subject from an operational viewpoint as well as an aesthetic one it opens up a wider understanding of the genre and the challenges faced in reaching built solutions.

This is not a straightforward field of architecture, as those involved will testify. While architectural historians may be critical of the design of many more recent railway buildings, it is hoped that the background story of those involved through all periods of railway history will be of value to those with an interest in this branch of architecture and how it has manifested itself over the years of diverse operational management imperatives and cultural context.

The story of railway development naturally breaks down into generally accepted chronological divisions and these have been used throughout, but it should

The restoration of St Pancras Station, London, to accommodate international train services perfectly illustrates the magnificence of railway architecture at its grandest. The imaginative reuse of hitherto unseen parts of the building and the exemplary conservation work amply demonstrate the part the past has to play in the future. (Photo: Paul Childs)

perhaps be noted that architectural fashions and trends do not wholly align with this breakdown:

1. Pioneering Victorian 1825 to 1870
2. Later Victorian and Edwardian including World War I (1870–1922)
3. Railway Grouping including World War II (1923–47)
4. Nationalization 1947–94
5. Privatization 1994–2019 and beyond.

The text and examples generally cited constrain themselves to those buildings that once supported or are now supporting mainline railway companies and their operations rather than, for instance, those

commercial buildings located on or adjacent to sites even where their form may have been influenced or constrained by the peculiarities of railway operations. Nevertheless, these have occasionally produced characterful and distinctive architecture in its own right. Witness, for example, the oversite developments at Charing Cross or Liverpool Street.

The book is aimed at all those with an interest in the design of railway buildings of any type and particularly those with an interest in the practice of architecture in the railway environment. It is hoped that it will appeal to architects and designers, engineers, railway enthusiasts, social historians and to the general reader who may have no prior knowledge of railways or the rich, complex and varied history that

Embankment Place, designed by Terry Farrell and Company Ltd and completed in 1991, sits directly over and spans the platforms at Charing Cross Station. The influence of the railway operations below is uniquely expressed in the form and outlook of the building. (Photo: Robert Thornton)

is embodied or manifest in its structures, buildings, landscapes and cityscapes.

It is written by those with first-hand experience of working both as practitioners and 'clients' in the railway industry and acknowledges the operational, practical and commercial pressures typically brought to bear on projects of all scales and sizes within the industry. We hope to illustrate what railway building designers and architects have striven, and continue to strive, to achieve with their buildings on behalf of their company masters or clients.

Note that we have adopted acronyms for railway companies widely used by other railway architecture historians and authors and have omitted ampersands where they form part of a single company title, e.g London & North Western Railway becomes LNWR, and only re-introduced them where two railway companies have joined forces, e.g. Great Northern Great North Eastern Railway Joint becomes GN &GERJ'.

AfA	'Access for All'
BM	Backlog Maintenance Programme
BR	British Rail(ways)
BR	Bedford Railway
BREEAM	Building Research Establishment Environmental Assessment Method
BER	Bristol & Exeter Railway
BR (E)	British Railways Eastern Region
BR (M)	British Railways London Midland Region
BR (Sc)	British Railways Scottish Region
BR (S)	British Railways Southern Region
BRUTE	British Railways Universal Trolley Equipment
BR (W)	British Railways Western Region
BTC	British Transport Commission
CR	Caledonian Railway
CHR	Chester & Holyhead Railway
CLASP	Consortium of Local Authorities Special Programme
DB	Deutsche Bahn
DAD	Director of Architecture & Design
DADE	Director of Architecture Design & Environment
D70	Design for the 1970s
ECR	Eastern Counties Railway
FfR	Ffestiniog Railway
GSWR	Glasgow & South Western Railway
GRC	Glass reinforced concrete / cement
GRP	Glass reinforced plastic
GJR	Grand Junction Railway
GCR	Great Central Railway
GER	Great Eastern Railway
GN & GERJ	Great Northern & Great Eastern Railway Joint
GNR	Great Northern Railway
GWR	Great Western Railway (1837 - 1948)

HWR	Hereford & Worcester Railway
HS1	High Speed 1
HR	Highland Railway
HMR & CC	Huddersfield Manchester Railway & Canal Co
IC	InterCity
IBR	Ipswich & Bury Railway
LCR	Lancaster & Carlisle Railway
LMR	Liverpool & Manchester Railway
LBR	London & Birmingham Railway
LGR	London & Greenwich Railway
LNER	London & North Eastern Railway
LNW & LYJ	London & North Western and Liverpool & Yorkshire Joint
LNWR	London & North Western Railway
LSWR	London & South Western Railway
LSR	London & Southampton Railway
LBSCR	London Brighton & South Coast Railway
LCDR	London Chatham & Dover Railway
LMSR	London Midland & Scottish Railway
MSLR	Manchester Sheffield & Lincolnshire Railway
MR	Midland Railway
NEC	National Exhibition Centre
NSIP	National Stations Improvement Programme
NSE	Network SouthEast
NCR	Newcastle & Carlisle Railway
NBR	North British Railway
NER	North Eastern Railway
NMR	North Midlands Railway
NSR	North Staffordshire Railway
O D70	Office Design for 1970s
RTC	Railway Technical Centre, Derby
RAT-TRAD	Rationalized traditional
RIBA	Royal Institute of British Architects
SNCF	Société Nationale des Chemin de Fers (Francais)
SECR	South Eastern & Chatham Railway
SER	South Eastern Railway
SWR	South Wales Railway
SR	Southern Railway
SRP	Station Regeneration Programme
SDR	Stockton & Darlington Railway
SPR	Syston & Peterborough Railway
TVR	Taff Vale Railway
TSI-PRM	Technical Specification for Interoperability - Standards for Persons with Reduced Mobility
TOC	Train Operating company
TVR	Trent Valley Railway
WHR	West Highland Railway
WLR	West Lancashire Railway
YNMR	York & North Midlands Railway

Part 1: The Inheritance

Chapter One

Railway Buildings Today

An Aged and Architecturally Rich Operational Estate

When looking at current or former railway buildings, the observer is presented with a complex living history of the genesis and development of the railway system, which embraces the architectural fashions, whims and peccadillos of all those responsible for the production of its buildings in each period of railway history. This history is sometimes eventful, turbulent and often controversial and it provides a rich tapestry of artefacts, most of which, unlike many more recent bland structures, can be dated and attributed to specific architects, engineers and contractors or privately commissioned consultants.

Although a modern transportation network relies on up-to-date engineering and operational technology, the railway buildings in the UK comprise an eclectic mix of structures representing nearly two centuries of engineering and architectural prowess, progress and pioneering development. This lengthy timeline does have its consequences today though and it is against the sometimes conflicting mix of modern operations and historic infrastructure that the buildings should be

Most station buildings reflect periods of change, development and civic context. Here at Reading the new platform access deck, designed by Grimshaw and opened in 2012, is located adjacent to the second station built on this site in 1868, which replaced Isambard Kingdom Brunel's 1840 station. (Photo: Jon Cunningham)

viewed, as this presents not insubstantial challenges in respect of costs and operational practicalities.

The buildings and underlying infrastructure that support the current train services and passenger activities are, in the main, the legacy of the nineteenth century. However, unlike the core engineering structures such as bridges, viaducts and tunnels, the basic elements of which are often still capable of fulfilling modern needs without deleterious impact on their appearance, these buildings have often been significantly altered, adapted, replaced or removed as the nature and scale of railway operations has progressed through its historic phases. This same need for change and development continues today.

The operational railways 'estate' as it now stands is unique in its engineering make-up and building stock. Although other large property and landowners perhaps have more historic portfolios with buildings ranging over a wider period of history, the railway estate is the only one with physical continuity and connectivity across the entire country. This unique attribute contributes significantly to its architectural character. In addition to the operational buildings, there are also many former railway buildings across the country that have found themselves unwanted due to system cutbacks or unusable because their functionality is no longer relevant to contemporary operations. Together these combine to represent every manner of architectural development, both evolutionary and revolutionary. Many buildings, such as stations, embraced the architectural influences and manners extant at the time of building, but many represent and reflect entirely new building requirements such as signal boxes, carriage and wagon works, and locomotive roundhouses.

Architectural Styles and Diversity

The operational infrastructure of today is a complex mix of structures and buildings of all types mainly dating from the early nineteenth century onwards although there are also earlier buildings in the portfolio where, for instance, they were inherited by railway

companies from the canal companies they acquired in the course of their business.

For many, the words 'railway architecture' conjure up images of grand Victorian or Edwardian terminals or country stations resplendent with wrought-iron filigree. Indeed, stations are probably the most familiar of railway buildings, but there has often been an equal, or greater, number of other operational buildings to accommodate supporting operations. These may include administrative offices, signal boxes, motive power and maintenance depots, warehouses, hotels, lineside buildings, water towers, sub-stations, control rooms, dockside buildings and so on. In the second half of the twentieth century, the range of building types expanded to embrace such facilities as computer systems operations centres, research establishments and even a hoverport terminal.

The railway buildings making up the 'operational' estate today represent only a small percentage of the total number of buildings created for railway purposes over the period of its history. Many buildings have come out of operational use as a result of cutbacks to the system or technological development, thus the demise of steam engine roundhouses and the reduction in the number of signal boxes. Fortunately, however, good representative examples of these still exist as other uses have been found for them. They were not all necessarily of great architectural quality, but many were robust and of historic interest. The multi-level stable at Paddington is a typical example; in use now as laboratory accommodation for the adjacent hospital, it once housed and cared for nearly 400 horses in service to the Great Western Railway (GWR) until as late as the 1940s.

The scale of the operational portfolio continues to ebb and flow but whilst the number of buildings has diminished over the last hundred years there are now new buildings being added to suit modern management methods. It is perhaps regrettable that, as well as those already mentioned, other operationally specific buildings such as depot control towers, water towers, transhipment sheds and motor vehicle workshops and so on, that were designed to serve the inner workings

Robert Stephenson's tubular iron bridge over the River Conwy is in a particularly sensitive setting adjacent to both the castle and Thomas Telford's suspension bridge. The bridge abutments were designed in conjunction with Francis Thompson to integrate with the medieval walls alongside which the tracks run. (Photo: Robert Thornton)

of the railway no longer exist to illustrate a bigger picture of the railway architectural story. Whilst it is possible to lament the passing of many wonderful station buildings, one should not perhaps forget the development of these more esoteric buildings, the purpose for which no longer exists.

It should also be noted that, whilst specifically designed for the railway system, railway operations also impact on, and are associated with many historic sites of greater age, such as the periphery of Conwy Castle and aspects of Hadrian's Wall in Newcastle. Not only this but the estate comprises many monuments, sculptures and artworks too. The lines and associated infrastructure are also often situated in areas of outstanding natural beauty or conservation areas and take on a different meaning in this context.

Victorian architectural and engineering detailing tends to dominate the historic building stock of the railways and traditional or revivalist building techniques were generally adopted for buildings during the first half of the twentieth century. However, a number of architectural fashions have been adopted since, ranging from International modernism, 'hi-tech', brutalism and postmodern to rationalised traditional,

'eco' and today's, yet to be identified, eclectic and esoteric mix.

The bulk of the infrastructure was set down in the nineteenth century with the consequence that the opportunity to create entirely new buildings at any subsequent period did not present itself very often if at all. New elements, such as station canopies or parts of station buildings have been constructed within existing sites, but to some these do not necessarily sit comfortably with their hosts; they do, however, add a further storyline to the history of the premises.

Despite the impact of developing technology and digitization on all aspects of operations, and notwithstanding the major changes already occurring in the signalling world, the range of buildings required to support railway operations is not likely to change significantly in the near future. However, the growth in the passenger business, leading to the need for new stations or the expansion of existing ones is a key driving force in the early part of the twenty-first century.

Scale of Operations and Architecture

Over the first century of railway operations, the amount of land acquired, and the number of buildings created, rendered the railway industry 'estate' one of the biggest in the UK. Later aerial photographs of the great works at Swindon, Doncaster, Crewe, York and Glasgow amply demonstrate this. Whilst the amount of land in railway use has been much reduced from its maximum extent prior to World War I, this still makes it one of the largest estates in the UK alongside the National Trust, the Crown, the Ministry of Defence, Highways England, the Forestry Commission and the Church Commissioners.

Few people would be familiar with the range of buildings and the scale of the land needed to support rail operations, much of which would be hidden from view by high walls with carefully controlled access points. Whilst these sites generally contained utilitarian buildings, they often, nonetheless, embraced buildings of architectural and now industrial archaeological interest.

A feel for the scale of these operations can now be experienced following the opening up of former railway sites and yards, such as those at Swindon and now particularly at King's Cross where the 135 acres (55 hectares) of former railway land north of St Pancras and King's Cross stations has gradually been converted into contemporary uses whilst simultaneously exposing and exhibiting the very best of the historic architectural qualities this site has to offer. Many buildings within the works footprint at Swindon have been demolished but a number of key buildings remain, notably the Chief Mechanical Engineer's building by Isambard Kingdom Brunel. Some of the remaining workshops have been converted into a retail outlet and offices where the historic structures add significant character to the user experience.

A glance at the statistics related to route mileage and the number of stations spread across the land at three critical periods in their development may help to explain the requirements for buildings and the demands placed on them. At the peak extent of the railway network in the early years of the twentieth century the route mileage of track reached nearly 20,000mi (32,187km) and by the time of the Beeching report – *The Reshaping of British Railways* – released in 1962, this figure had been reduced to 17,830mi (28,695km). As a consequence of adopting the recommendations of the report, this mileage further reduced to approximately 10,000mi (16,000km) where it remains to this day. Over the same benchmark periods the number of stations dropped from approximately 9,000 in 1914 to 7,000 in 1962. The number of passenger stations closed after the Beeching

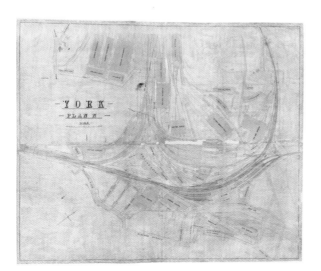

The plan of the railway works in York in the pioneer years of railway development illustrates the scale and extent of the enterprise, which was repeated at a number of centres – usually midway along key routes. Each site had major implications for employment and the demands for specialized buildings.

report numbered 2,363 although 435 of these were already under consideration of closure or, indeed, already closed beforehand. The operational stations on the network now number more than 2,500. The discrepancy in the figures related to station closures is explained by the fact that the word 'station' was also applied to freight and goods-only premises in historic records.

Until the general adoption of 'train-load' freight rather than 'wagon-load' freight, stations were very much multi-purpose and often embraced goods sheds, coal depots, animal pens – sometimes including nearby abattoirs – and sundry other offices concerned with the upkeep and maintenance of the railway infrastructure and its rolling stock in the vicinity of the station.

Whilst the closure of a large number of stations may appear alarming it should be pointed out that they were not all of significant architectural quality: many were halts with short platforms and rudimentary forms of shelter, although it is known, of course, that there were a number of important casualties. Whether those with recognized architectural qualities would have survived, had they been preserved for consideration in our current era where 'heritage' is more highly valued by the industry and the communities it serves, is a moot point.

In relationship to the scale of the enterprise, it is also interesting to note that manpower requirements have changed significantly in the industry and these have a major implication for buildings of all types whether they be administrative offices, manufactories, carriage and wagon works, signal boxes or the many other specific activities related to rail operations. Up to the time of the nationalization there were approximately 650,000 staff in the employ of railway companies, and this had reduced to just under 475,000 by 1962 to be further reduced in stages to under 150,000 just prior to the privatization of 1994.

The railway 'estate' has seen growth and contraction over its period of operation in both usage and the physical infrastructure required to meet demand, but these two aspects have not always been analogous. After unpredicted growth in passenger travel following privatization, the passenger figures approximate to a doubling of demand over the twenty years since the new millennium and, at the time of writing, the forecast predicts a further doubling in the next twenty-five years. It is interesting to note that these figures are at their highest since the post-World War II period when there were more than twice the number of stations to accommodate travellers. The increase in passenger numbers not only affects the size and scale of station premises, but also requires more frequent and longer trains which in turn has further consequences for the infrastructure. Handling more people safely often requires wider and longer platforms, which may, in turn, require new footbridges linking the platforms, works to embankments and bridge abutments where station lengths are constrained by them, and changes to signalling and track layouts.

Pressures on railway operations and on the supporting buildings are still expected to grow. In 2017 overall usage was 4.5 million passengers per day but this is expected to grow by 100 per cent by 2041 with freight growth expected to be in the region of 90 per cent. Assessing the impact of this growth on railway premises requires sophisticated modelling techniques to ensure adequate spatial capacity and the safety and comfort of passengers.

Railway Management Influence on Design

It is inevitable that the management of the railway system and all its constituent functions has a major impact on the need for buildings and the design of them, but often it is overlooked that the style and method of management during the key historic periods also has an impact on the resultant architecture, even if not intentionally.

The railway industry as a whole has involved the services of architects and other railway building designers in a number of ways over its history and this process continues to change as design and construction methodologies change. The shift from the use of a diverse selection of private practitioners and consultants through the early Victorian period to the build-up of 'in-house' resources through the later Victorian and Edwardian, Grouping and nationalized periods and back again following privatization has had a tangible influence on the development of architectural styles, detailing and production methodology – the latter now being rather euphemistically labelled as 'delivery'.

The number of consultants active in the nineteenth century and working for the many train companies produced many individualistic pieces of architecture, albeit with their own characteristic flourishes and often used before on other public, civic or ecclesiastical buildings. When railway companies amalgamated or expanded to the point where they found it more economic to recruit salaried staff, the individual flair started to be eroded and former building plans became templates for further work and an approach to standardization.

With notable exceptions it is generally clear from the design of railway buildings to which period they belong, not just by architectural 'fashion' but by such things as the utilization of practical architectural details or the repetition of elements.

The Victorian era was dominated by revivalist styles coupled with engineering prowess and display; the Edwardian period by the standardization of traditional forms and the Grouping period by the quest for modernity and the railway company's ambition to express speed and glamour. The nationalized period presented the first opportunity for railway management to express a national intent and identity for its services and the subsequent privatized era gave free reign to the new railway company managers to express their services via the design of their buildings and interiors to suit their target customers.

However, there is much that was modern about the buildings of the Grouping period and which also demonstrated a stronger centralized control of design direction, particularly in the drive for standardization of design approach if not always in detailing. The later privatized period is, however, a bit of a hybrid as, whilst the infrastructure company that 'delivers' most of the buildings engages many diverse consultants, it does endeavour to produce standards and consistency of design in the interests of its maintenance and longer-term sustainability aspirations. A relatively short period within the nationalized era was, in fact, the only time when architecture had an opportunity to be standardized across the entire country but apart from a 'corporate identity' applied to graphics and industrial design this wasn't really applied to a building programme. Yes, there was a standard approach to such things as ticket office layouts and the purchase of related, specialized furniture, but this principle did not find a national form in respect of buildings, each regional architect's team or project architect still having the freedom to develop an individual style in the spirit of the national goal.

To those familiar with the possibilities of a coherent central design direction in the nationalized era, the fragmentation of the privatized era might appear to be a retrograde step particularly when comparisons are made to, say, Deutsche Bahn (DB) or Societé Nationale des Chemins de Fer Français (SNCF) which have retained strength of identity nationally.

The strength and coherence of railway design management in the UK is of a changeable nature but the shift has definitely been away from 'in-house' resources to the management of external consultants since the mid-1990s. This, in effect, reflects more closely the prevalent process of design management prior to the 1922 Grouping when favoured consultant practices, led by such eminent architects as Charles Henry Driver, Francis Thompson, David Mocatta and Matthew Digby Wyatt, were at their zenith. There are now many architectural practices involved in the design of railway buildings and of course these have built up their own expertise, which in some cases has enabled them to work in an international field.

The privatized era also sees the gradual shift in emphasis towards 'design and build' throughout the industry with the 'client' railway companies generally favouring the appointment of contractor's teams embracing all design discipliners and responding to the client via project management teams. The professional architects in the client companies, where appointed, now manage appropriate design standards and offer design review and approval services via the project management teams.

Stakeholders and Third Parties

When railway companies were entirely masters of their own destinies in terms of the design of the infrastructure they were building, the engineers and architects generally had free reign to express their engineering and architectural prowess without third-party direction or influence. This led to some of the most exciting and uncompromising artefacts that this country, or indeed the world, had seen before – and in some cases, since.

Whilst there are many architecturally interesting railway buildings away from public scrutiny, the design of stations has always been the focal point for the public's attention, and this is where the architecture is generally most expressive and responsive to current vogues, fashions and cultural influences.

The most contentious issues surrounding these buildings were generally to do with siting and location rather than design, as most of the land required for track and infrastructure needed to be purchased from established landowners, who were not necessarily keen on having their land bisected by railway lines and the attendant cuttings, embankments, bridges, viaducts and tunnels.

The 'stakeholders' in almost all architectural projects on the railways in the twenty-first century are great in number and have diverse interests. These range from the funders, who may not be the railway company responsible for undertaking the work, the local communities acting independently or through their local planning authorities, the national heritage bodies, the user groups and indeed all the other consultees that these groups refer to in the course of their deliberations.

It is acknowledged that railway buildings, particularly stations of historic interest, often have ancillary civic functions to satisfy and more recently the role of stations, in particular, is seen as a potential catalyst for regeneration and the key to the development of sustainable communities supported by a wide range of stakeholders.

The architects and their immediate points of contact in respect of their instruction are left to interpret many diverse requirements, objectives and aspirations whilst still keeping an eye on cost, programme and, ultimately, the quality of the job and the need to meet all the functional objectives of the project. This is surely the most difficult of tasks in today's climate when the inevitable overriding economies are also to be made.

The Great Western Railway routed through Bath cut through Sydney Gardens, a key promenade area but was designed in such a way as to celebrate and display the new steam train services and thus placate those affected by the changes to this popular location. (Photo: Robert Thornton)

Chapter Two

The Heritage

Age and Consequences

The underlying formation and infrastructure of the railways generally dates from the middle decades of the nineteenth century. Whilst there are many buildings of later date representing all styles and manners of architecture, the core station buildings serving railway operations tend to date from the later decades of the nineteenth century as many of the original stations required rebuilding as rail traffic grew at an unprecedented pace. Not only is the infrastructure this aged, but it was predominantly laid down within a relatively short period in two recognized 'manias' of building between 1830 and 1875. The scale and rapidity of this enterprise is the more astonishing when one considers that it was embracing pioneering technology.

The consequence of this is that much of what is visible today is made up of Victorian and Edwardian buildings with fewer representative buildings of the second half of the twentieth century, although this balance is being redressed to a degree by new projects now on stream or awaiting commissioning. The bridges, tunnels, cuttings and embankments that are familiar to all rail users generally appear as built but, of course, have been modified or maintained in a manner commensurate with twenty-first century operations. It is a testimony to the quality of the underlying engineering that so much of what was created in the railway building boom periods remains in use – albeit not always for railway operations – despite the intensity of the railway traffic that now runs over, under or through it.

Where they remain, the buildings, in comparison,

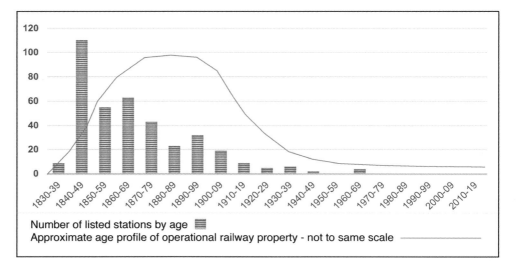

This diagram provides an approximate guide to the age profile of railway buildings still in operational use. It also indicates where the conservation interests have been focused, bearing in mind that this activity only gained momentum in the second half of the twentieth century. (Credit: Robert Thornton)

Number of listed stations by age
Approximate age profile of operational railway property - not to same scale

have often been altered or decommissioned whereby their original character or meaning is lost. Nearly all existing railway buildings, certainly stations, have been modified in each of the periods identified and this is reflected in their visual make-up. This is particularly noticeable in the larger premises such as Paddington Station, which encompasses the 1852 building – itself a replacement for the original 1839 station, the 1916 additional vault, the 1930s offices and platform extensions, the 1990s 'Lawn' remodelling, the 2015 taxi facility and new Hammersmith and City line interchange, the 2017 further updating of the 'Lawn' and the major rebuilding of the former departure side of the station to form the interchange with the newly constructed Crossrail station. Manchester Piccadilly is another such a hybrid and comprises fully operational buildings dating from the 1860s (the three-span shed), the 1960s (the suburban platforms and the tower block) and the 1990s (the concourse and Metro Station).

Such buildings thus represent and reflect multiple periods of architecture and the cultural context of each of the periods within which they were altered. For this reason, there is a rich 'archaeology' to be experienced or explored in most railway buildings.

This engineering and architectural inheritance very much informs the current asset-management policy of the infrastructure owners and operators, which has to take account of many assessments of the remaining useful life of any particular asset, especially where condition and functional capability might impact on operational safety. These considerations do not just relate to buildings and structures but, importantly, the hidden aspects of earthworks, drainage and even lineside vegetation, although any failings here can of course have deleterious impacts on associated buildings.

Building Condition

Following the significant building repair and improvement work undertaken over the last twenty-five years, it is perhaps difficult to appreciate that the poor condition of railway buildings and the widespread experience of their down-at-heel appearance, particularly after World War II, was leading to a nationally felt desire for significant renewal, particularly by those responsible for their safety and maintenance. This motivated some improvements in the British Railways modernization plan of the 1950s but also informed many of the closures and the demolitions that followed the failings of this initiative during the 1960s and early 1970s.

The overall impression of railway buildings and particularly stations now is of an architecturally interesting, generally well-maintained infrastructure. Of course, there are poor examples but if one compares images of, for instance, the major stations struggling through the 1950s, 1960s and 1970s to the same examples seen now, the comparison is startling.

One aspect of architectural appreciation that our current generation is largely unaware of, but which had a significant impact on the assessment of Victorian and Edwardian architecture in later periods, is that the industrial developments that accompanied and sustained the growth of the national economy, and indeed the transport system in these periods, were fuelled by coal. This led to the settlement of thick layers of carbon over many edifices, particularly in urban areas. This deposit was so thick that fine details of architectural expression could be completely hidden, and essential building qualities lost to view. Whilst the architectural qualities of strong forms such as Huddersfield or Monkwearmouth stations could still be discerned, it was perhaps more difficult to appreciate the qualities of lesser railway buildings.

This aspect of architecture, which is little discussed now, was partly responsible for the widespread public view that most Victorian architecture existing after World War II represented an out of date and ugly response to our building needs. This attitude culminated in a tidal wave of renewal, slum clearance and general freshening up of the urban environment after

Waterloo concourse in 2019 with (inset) a similar view from the 1970s. The light-coloured paving installed in the 1980s heralded a major change in the visual quality of station environments. At Waterloo, this included a fully restored roof in the 1990s and the later addition of a gallery to provide more space and facilities for passengers.

post-war austerity.

Whilst many visual improvements came about from the mid-1970s onwards and gained momentum in the business-sector-led railway of the 1980s onwards, one of the biggest changes in the fortunes of railway buildings came about after privatization with the government-funded Station Regeneration Programme (SRP) which saw, over a six-year period, significant improvement to over 2,000 stations. This in itself had been preceded by a 'Backlog Maintenance' programme which was intended to address the underlying causes of many buildings' failures and poor performance such as broken drainage systems, failing building services systems and urgent roof repairs.

The work undertaken as part of the SRP kick-started a number of other projects at the premises in the confidence that the underlying infrastructure would not let the project down at a later date. It is easy to now take for granted the massive improvement this project made to the overall impression of the station environment but perhaps more than any other single project it brought into sharp relief the quality of the architectural inheritance.

Despite the widespread good done by the SRP project there were still a number of station premises that fell through the net, either as a result of 'planning blight' or the promise of a replacement project that would solve all ills but did not happen for one reason or another. Some of these were highlighted in the 2009 report to government entitled *Better Stations*. Fortunately, the very worst station identified in the report, Wakefield Kirkgate, has now been brought back into line, with a multi-stakeholder package of

improvements, a model that is now becoming more commonplace as local communities take more of a part in the planning and development of their local stations.

Fitness for Purpose

The age, design and condition of the existing buildings in the railway estate has a major impact on the management and development of it to meet the current and future needs of railway companies, especially where the existing buildings affected by proposals have statutory protection or where local community or national interests play a part.

Unlike the situation during the 1950s and 1960s where the buildings were often worn out, rotting or surplus to requirements, the biggest challenge to those developing the estate now is not one of condition but one of fitness for purpose and, of course, commercial and operational performance.

Whilst the core purpose of the railway system in terms of the transportation of goods and people

remains as originally intended, the organizational and logistical structure that placed specific building requirements on it has changed significantly over time. For example, the changes in the methodology of maintaining and repairing trains, the storage and trans-shipment of goods such as coal and corn, the development of different means of signalling and so on, have all premeditated the redundancy of many building types such as engine sheds, warehouses, depots and signal boxes.

Changing Attitudes

The condition and visual state of existing railway buildings after World War II was one of the aspects felt to be holding back the fortunes of the railway system and modernization and streamlining was seen by some as essential to its survival. This attitude, coupled with the operational closures accelerated by the adoption of the proposals put forward by the then Chairman of BR, Dr Beeching, in 1962, triggered a preservationist mood amongst those who cared for buildings affected by these proposals.

The closures of lines in the mid to late 1960s left many stations and their attendant buildings looking for new uses, being boarded up to await purchase or being demolished. The threat to many such buildings was of deep concern to those who cherished and wanted to preserve them.

The major cultural and political differences expressed during the 1960s and the early 1970s in relation to railway heritage following the destruction of the Euston Arch, such that it could not be relocated or re-erected, together with the desire to demolish St Pancras have both ignited and fortified a heritage protection movement that has had implications far beyond the railway industry and the United Kingdom. It is possible that many more worthy buildings might have been lost later if these battles had not served to demonstrate so publicly the opposing positions of those proposing such destruction and those against it.

The latter years of the 1960s and the early years of the 1970s did not allay the fears of those who saw the gradual deterioration of the existing building stock and did not sympathetically view the attempts to rebuild and renew elements of the system. However, when viewed from the 2000s, those days seem a long way off, and the railway industry has seen a massive transformation of its building stock in terms of condition, quality and functionality. During this same period there has also been a shift in public perception of the qualities of railway buildings, particularly stations. The fears of conservationists, so very well-articulated by groups such as 'Save Britain's Heritage' in the 1970s have, to a great extent, been averted, but there has also been unpredicted growth in railway patronage which has, to a degree, taken away the need to further pare down the system and its intrinsic historic content whilst putting different sorts of pressures on existing buildings. Some will argue that were it not for the 'modernization' and streamlining of the network there would be many more good examples but others will point out that were it not for the essential pruning and changes brought about by a corporate approach, more of the buildings would have become redundant and faced an uncertain future.

It is perhaps understandable that the rift between those who wanted to move into a brave new world in the fifties and sixties and those who wanted to preserve the intrinsic qualities of the historic estate grew wider until the showdowns of the 1970s, but certainly since then attitudes have changed. Perhaps the real turning point came in the 1980s when the newly appointed chairman of BR, Sir Peter Parker, publicly acknowledged that architectural heritage was important to the rail business.

Following very successful and sustainable projects that integrated contemporary operational

Similar in scale and architectural detail to London's St Pancras, the former Manchester Central Station was one of the first large stations to find a new use in the middle of a city. Listed Grade II in 1963, it finally closed as a railway building in 1969 after rail services were withdrawn two years earlier. EGS Design were the architects for the conversion, which was completed in 1983. (Photo: Robert Thornton)

The water tower at Inverness locomotive shed would surely have been regarded as a gem of a building now. It was away from public gaze and yet its functionality straddling the track and its siting as a gateway to the shed gave it a classical stance and dignity fitting of a more civic location. (Drawing: Robert Thornton)

requirements into historic contexts at stations such as Glasgow Central, Manchester Piccadilly, Liverpool Street and later at Paddington, St Pancras and King's Cross, this is no longer the extremely sensitive issue that it was forty or so years ago, although there will always be instances where the proposals of railway companies and their appointed designers do not find favour with specific interest groups.

Lost Heritage

Whilst the operational railway buildings are mainly administered by the current main infrastructure company, Network Rail, railway buildings are widely dispersed amongst many owners, including heritage railway companies. Tracking the extent, location and fortunes of former operational buildings is therefore a little difficult but can be a rewarding exercise.

Many of the buildings that historically gave the railway property portfolio its collective character, but found themselves no longer needed for operational purposes, have either been demolished, fallen into disrepair or have had new uses found

for them. Accepting that station losses are reasonably well recorded, it is not known precisely how many other buildings have disappeared. Whilst these may not have been architecturally distinctive, they would, nevertheless, have displayed a robustness, style and character unique to the railway system. The English Heritage publication, *Lost Railways*, by John Minnis, highlights the significance of many of these buildings.

Whilst buildings such as the Euston Arch and the earlier Birmingham New Street Station were well-known casualties, there are many other less well-known buildings that have suffered this fate, possibly because they were away from the public domain or gaze, such the grand water tower at Inverness locomotive shed or the roundhouse at Stoke works, both of which would surely have been highly regarded and protected now.

Perhaps the biggest changes to the scale of the railway enterprise, though, relate to the many building sites that once made up the manufactories and maintenance establishments that each of the railway companies built up. The end of the nationalized period saw the demise of the core activities on these sites and the once-great works at the hearts of the railway regions finally closed down. The works at Swindon, York, Doncaster and Crewe have, for instance, all become redundant as the manufacturing process either reduced in scale or moved into the premises of private contractors.

Other changes to the need for, or use of, railway buildings in the post-war period have come about as a result of the development of other forms of transport, particularly the use of road transport for the distribution of commodities such as coal and vegetables. The nationalized period saw the closure of many large goods yards in major cities, such as Somers Town adjacent to St Pancras and the coal drops in King's Cross yard. The need for motive power depots, water towers, turntables, coaling stations and so on, all disappeared with the demise of steam. As a result of the introduction of diesel traction and electrification, faster journey times also led the way to the demise of hostels provided for steam-train drivers at the end of their shifts. Bearing in mind the siting of many of these buildings, finding new uses for them was always going to be difficult and many did not survive.

The combination of closures and the changes in operational requirements during the 1960s has been seen by some as the polar opposite of the 'Railway Mania' of the nineteenth century and, indeed, a mania in its own right.

Reuse and Regeneration

It is clear that had many of the buildings demolished in the 1960s and 1970s survived to a later period, a different view would have been taken as to their future. Experience over recent years has shown that historic railway buildings can find new life as interesting premises for a wide range of activities, and indeed become the springboard for the regeneration of an area. The pioneering work at the Camden Roundhouse in the 1960s, and the former Manchester Central Station, showed what could be done before such enterprises became mainstream.

Adaptation is now more widespread and whilst many former railway buildings are no longer needed to serve the railway, they more commonly survive through reuse as commercial facilities such as concert venues, retail merchants or restaurants, for example the former Leeds 'roundhouse' and the goods shed at Canterbury West Station. Unfortunately, whilst the latter is a good example of reuse of that type of building, it has possibly only survived because it is easily accessible on foot within an urban environment. Those goods sheds located more remotely or in inaccessible locations besides operational railway lines are less fortunate.

The bigger sites are more problematic and require significant multi-disciplinary, multi-stakeholder master-planning activities such as those in hand at King's Cross, Swindon and York. The scale of such sites as Swindon highlighted the difficulties inherent in regenerative activities at certain periods, and the closure of the works amidst the economic difficulties of the 1970s was not conducive to swift development. Fortunately, the most important of the remaining buildings were saved and have provided accommodation for a range of activities including a museum, headquarters offices and a major retail outlet.

It is perhaps fortunate, on reflection, that the development of what was known as the King's Cross Railway Lands remained commercially unviable for so long and that so many of the historically valuable buildings on its 135 acres (55 hectares) remained intact to become the heart of a thriving new quarter that takes its character from these buildings. Work is still in progress as part of a longer-term development plan following the reopening of St Pancras as the second international terminal in 2004.

Reuse of railway buildings is far more widespread now and this gives clues as to how further regeneration might take place and be attractive to a wider audience. Good examples are demonstrated by the conversion of the water-tank facilities and supporting building at Huddersfield Station, which has now been converted into a viable office complex. Similarly, the former water-storage facility at Settle has been successfully converted into a private residence.

The former goods shed at Canterbury West Station is a fine example of the imaginative reuse of a former railway building where the character and purpose of the original building is still evident and a fitting background to the farmers' market and restaurant, aptly named the Goods Shed, that now thrive within. (Photo: Robert Thornton)

The rugged charm of railway buildings is now recognized as providing the potential to become the focus of regeneration and there are many such examples of this around the UK where these are developed in conjunction with local communities. Stations are particularly successful in this endeavour, as they deliver a ready-made user group for commercial facilities to take advantage of. More recent planning strategies that recognize the sustainable nature of such juxtapositions have assisted greatly in this success, Sheaf Square in Sheffield being one such example. Whilst they are not all on the same scale as the redevelopment of the King's Cross railway lands, many communities see the potential of the contribution that such buildings can make.

Railway Heritage

It is already noted that railway buildings and structures form an important part of Britain's architectural, social and cultural heritage and, as such, many of them are protected by listed status or sit within conservation areas. On the mainline operational railway network there are estimated to be more than 1,500 buildings and structures within such listings, and which are sometimes also associated with ancient monuments, such as those already mentioned at Hadrian's Wall in Newcastle and Conwy Castle in Gwynedd and also at Rewley Abbey in Oxford. Many are also associated with local listing or embrace Tree Preservation Orders. The largest grouping of listed locations generally date from the late nineteenth

Sheaf Square in Sheffield combines significant improvements to passenger facilities within the station and major improvements to the surrounding public domain, creating a fitting gateway to Sheffield and forming the heart of regeneration in the city centre. (Photo: Robert Thornton)

century, which perhaps, not unexpectedly, returns the highest proportion of the underlying building stock. This status adds to the complexity of managing such premises, particularly in an operational environment, where safety or other operational imperatives may be a critical factor, the implications of which may be in conflict with heritage driven aspirations.

Listing has come relatively recently in respect of railway history, and it is interesting to note that the first station was listed in 1951 and that this number had only risen to 20 by the end of the 1960s. The 1970s was possibly seen as a period of threat, and by the mid-decade a further 110 had been listed. SAVE Britain's Heritage identified these in their booklet *Off the Rails* published to coincide with the exhibition at the Royal Institute of British Architects (RIBA), Saving Railway Architecture, in 1977 and which served to highlight the threat to railway buildings at that time. Ten years on, the figure had risen to 280 and, at the time of writing, the figure stood at more than 400 operational station and many more former stations in private ownership. The trend for listing viaducts, bridges and other railway structures follows a similar growth pattern but attention is usually drawn to station buildings, particularly those that form the heart of local communities.

One might have expected that the rate of listing would have increased in the immediate aftermath of the destruction of the Euston Arch but although there was some change at this time the biggest rate of increase was to take place in the early 1970s and mid-1980s. It is not clear whether this is when the biggest threats to the buildings occurred or whether there was a corresponding change in the national mood to reflect a greater appreciation of the past.

What might now be more worrying is the pressure that the less recognized buildings are under, particularly those that were not regarded as great architecture when they were built and have subsequently been altered or defaced beyond redemption by thoughtless alterations, ill-considered installation of operational equipment and poor signage and so on, which now mask their original qualities.

In respect of the demonstration that heritage aspects of railway building are an integral part of their commercial allure and sustainability, the conversion of Liverpool Street Station in the City of London has led the way. The redevelopment of the station with heritage at its core in conjunction with a commercial property development finally demonstrated that the two aspects were not diametrically opposed and could sit comfortably together and, importantly, operate efficiently in a forward-looking railway. The identity that was forged through this project showed that stations of this age and architectural character could play a significant role in the regeneration and commercial attractiveness of a wider area. As a model this met all the criteria for a sustainable future and is also a great place to be. The fact that it was designed and delivered by British Rail's 'in-house' team of architects, engineers and project

Liverpool Street Station was dramatically remodelled between 1988 and 1992 when a new concourse and entrances to Liverpool Street and Bishopsgate were created with designs inspired by the original station details. (Photo: Paul Childs)

managers in the final years of the nationalized period is also perhaps not as well recognized as it should be.

The railway industry is now taking a much more proactive stance in relation to the listing of buildings within its ownership. It is inevitable that operational methodologies will change the way that railway companies manage their building stock and, in the case of Network Rail where there is, for instance, a need to operate the entire network with only a small number of control centres, the future of many signal boxes is in jeopardy. A proactive approach to the dilemma of de-commissioning and removing unwanted boxes from the operational environment was the subject of early consultation with the Local Planning and Heritage Authorities to ensure that the national interest was looked after. This commenced with a joint review of the entire portfolio of boxes to determine where protection should be applied, what measures should be put in place and what strategy should be used to relocate, dismantle or otherwise remove buildings from the operational estate.

Heritage Railways

There are over 100 standard and narrow-gauge 'heritage' railways in the UK. Most of the former were part of the BR network prior to the closures of the 1950s and 1960s. These play an important part in the history of railway architecture not only because many contain stations and ancillary buildings that are of interest in their own right but also because they can often become appropriate repositories for buildings and structures that find themselves redundant in current mainline operations. Redundant footbridges, signal boxes, turntables and small station buildings have all found their way onto these railways where they serve useful functions in 'period' settings. It should be noted, however, that the buildings attached to these railways usually set themselves in a specific period of steam-hauled travel and, of course, they are usually decorated and bedecked with equipment and paraphernalia to reflect that.

Sheringham Station on the North Norfolk Railway typifies the stations in the heritage movement and is an important visitor attraction for the town. It has recently been extended in traditional details by local architects Stead Mutton and Griggs and was highly commended in the National Railway Heritage Awards in 2016. (Photo: Robert Thornton)

Part 2: The Evolution of Railway Architecture

Genesis, Growth and Consolidation

Together, the Victorian and Edwardian periods saw the genesis, development and consolidation of the bulk of the railway system that is recognizable today. Indeed, as noted previously, the quality of the design of the infrastructure and its buildings dating from this period very much inform the asset management and investment policies of today.

From the opening of the Stockton & Darlington Railway in 1825, the railway network developed very quickly throughout Victoria's reign, and by 1870 the bulk of the railway network and its associated supporting infrastructure as we now know it had been put in place. Aside from the physical difficulties of achieving this, the legal difficulties and challenges encountered along the way in relation to land purchase and Parliamentary approvals only serve to show how determined the railway companies were to achieve their commercial aims.

The architectural output throughout this period was in the hands of consultants and building contractors commissioned directly by the railway companies, and generally the stylistic directions were left to them. Consequently, there are as many architectural styles as there were rail companies, architects and contractors engaged at any one time. Boundaries between engineering and architectural skills become blurred where architectural collaborations provide some of the most inspirational buildings of the period ranging from Paddington Station to the Britannia Bridge over the Menai Strait. It should also be remembered that as there were very few precedents for the types of buildings needed, many early buildings had to be rebuilt as, over time, their operational shortcomings became apparent.

Culham Station, Oxfordshire, opened in 1844 off Abingdon Road. It is a typical example of a Brunel roadside station, following the neo-Tudor style in red brick with stone dressings. (Photo: Malcolm Wood)

Bradford on Avon station, listed Grade II, is an example of early Brunel design in ashlar stone. The overhanging eaves and tall chimneys are a distinctive feature. It was constructed five years before the arrival of the railway. (Photo: Malcolm Wood)

Whilst the Victorian period saw massive growth of the system and pioneering engineering and building techniques emerged, the craft of building was still generally dominated by artisans and craftspeople using traditional techniques, even where, for instance, new types of structure or materials were introduced, for instance, patent-glazed roofing.

The rapid rise of the industry, with associated civic determination to be part of this revolution, saw many railway companies and local promoters keen to use the design services of recognized and respected architects, certainly for their public-facing buildings such as stations. In some circumstances, architects already in the pay of local landowners and dignitaries

were employed, possibly seen as a safe pair of hands, but also because they were in many cases already utilized as the driving forces behind local proposals, particularly where these might be contentious.

Whilst there was a great variety and freedom in the design of stations there was also a large amount of less prominent building work that generally followed established principles of other industrial buildings of the period now defined as the Industrial Revolution. The manufactories, workshops, depots, trans-shipment buildings and so on, developed an industrial aesthetic based on their own particular activities. The extent of these works grew rapidly as the railway companies expanded their manufacturing and

A fine detail of the proposed front elevation for Bath Spa Station from the office of Brunel in 1841. Note that the drawing is titled Bath Depot: terminology used at the time. (Drawing: Network Rail archive)

The Jacobean style of Worksop Station was attributed to James Drabble for the Manchester, Sheffield & Lincolnshire Railway (MS&LR). Opened in 1849, the extended frontage of the original main building is a feature of many larger country stations of the Victorian period. (Photo: Malcolm Wood)

maintenance capabilities. The size of the workforces needed to support them went as far as to create new settlements and, in one case, a new town at Crewe.

The great 'cathedral stations' and many other significant railway buildings and locations were founded in this early period and many of the larger stations saw rapid growth and alteration as the demand for railway travel and transportation grew. Fine architectural quality was extended to even the humblest of railway buildings, with architects and new-works engineers applying the same amount of design care on smaller yard buildings and goods sheds as would be expected on the most significant passenger-station building.

Over time there was development of a 'house' style for many railway companies, generally based on the design and form of buildings. This came partly from the use of repetitive design for specific elements, a feature that would become commonplace and a defining element of the railway environment in the later years of the nineteenth century. Whether this can be defined as being a 'railway architecture' style remains open to conjecture, as the architectural references used vary so widely, and were not necessarily pioneering in themselves, with styles ranging from an almost agricultural vernacular to ecclesiastical, classical and later 'Arts and Crafts' forms.

Within this period, the railways had grown to their maximum overall size and network coverage. However, the outbreak of the World War I, and the recovery from it, was to see an end to growth, indeed a gradual reduction in the extent of route mileage and the number of buildings needed to support the system.

James Miller developed Wemyss Bay (1903) with engineer Donald Matheson for the Caledonian Railway (CR) and was equally at home designing smaller Arts and Crafts stations, such as those on the West Highland Railway, as he was designing his well-known, larger buildings in Glasgow. (Photo: Malcolm Wood)

Chapter Three

The Pioneering Victorian Period – 1825–70

The Journey Begins

It is well established that the advent of the railways in the early part of the nineteenth century heralded one of the most significant periods of industrial and commercial development in the history of human enterprise. Not only were there rapid advances in the technological development of motive power and railway rolling stock, but also in the development of the related infrastructure with the consequential expansion and distribution of the communities served and connected. After the Rainhill Locomotive Trials of 1829, at which George Stephenson's 'Rocket' triumphed, and which proved that locomotive power could be successful, the railway industry started passenger services with confidence. This was despite warnings from doubters and opponents of the dire consequences that would result from travelling by train at speed. Even the earliest structures reflected an architectural approach that made a strong statement that the railway intended to be around for a considerable time, and which imbued a sense of confidence, strength and safety in its operations.

The buildings of the early period were based very much on local materials, or alternatively timber construction but, generally, the style of the buildings was left to the engineer of the route to decide, quite often taking the local vernacular into account. The architecture of lineside buildings was, within a few years, focused on the station's passenger facilities themselves as the elements intended to instill confidence.

The facilities ranged from simple but well-equipped station buildings with staff and waiting rooms to extremely basic lineside halts with little more than rudimentary weather protection. Some early stations were referred to in contemporary drawings as 'depots' and from that it is apparent that, even in the earliest years, goods facilities and accommodation for locomotives were also regarded as significant elements of the estate and, indeed, would eventually become the largest part in terms of building size and land requirements. The standard of finishes was dictated by economic considerations, but generally the construction of the shells of most buildings was established in either masonry or brickwork with roofs finished in slate or sheet metal such as zinc.

The Network of Railway Companies Spreads

It is worth taking a look at how railway buildings developed across the country, and from company to company in order to understand how building needs and solutions materialized alongside operational imperatives.

The Liverpool and Manchester Railway (LMR), opened in 1830 and certainly the first true 'intercity' route, overcame early operational limitations due to gradients by employing a cable-winding system between Liverpool and Edge Hill to draw trains to level track. The buildings constructed at Crown Street Station and at the winding engine housings at the building described as the 'Moorish Arch' were designed with a degree of solidity and civic gravitas.

Manchester Liverpool Road Station (1830), at the other extreme of the line, was designed with

Now an arts centre, the Grade II listed station at Edge Hill (architects Haig and Franklin for the Liverpool and Manchester Railway, 1836) replaced the original 1830 Crown Street Station and was extended as the cable-winding system was relocated. (Photo: Paul Childs)

a two-storey frontage, with rusticated details and entrances for first- and second-class passengers, and waiting facilities located on the upper floor at platform level. The architectural style of the building was elegant, yet simple.

Initially, the intermediate stations of the route featured steeply pitched gable roofs and neo-Tudor details for both door and window openings. The growth in popularity of the route engendered early examples of what would become common upgrades in 1842, when several locations were extended, including Earlestown and Rainhill.

In 1835, work was underway on construction of the London & Greenwich Railway (LGR). Colonel George Thomas Landmann RE (1779–1854), a military engineer of great experience, determined a route that was just over 3mi (5km) long, running from Southwark to Deptford. Two large inclined planes were to be constructed, one at London Bridge and the other at Deptford, to provide access to the railway, which, due to the marshy land alongside the River Thames, was carried on a high brick viaduct for the full length of the railway. Construction of the route was an immense draw on the supplies of Sittingbourne stock bricks, and the quality of the brickwork in the structure varied, depending

The original Liverpool and Manchester Railway station at Earlestown forms the main body of this building, which was extended in 1842 in a robust Gothic style and with a heavy canopy carried on sturdy columns, a detail repeated at Rainhill Station. (Photo: Malcolm Wood)

Colonnades of Doric columns are a key feature of the bridge at Spa Road, Bermondsey. This location was the original western terminus of the London & Greenwich Railway, which in 1836 was the first railway in London. (Photo: Paul Childs)

on the quality of the available bricks at the time. From 1836 the railway ran from a temporary station at Spa Road, Bermondsey, accessed from below a magnificent bridge with the spans supported by huge Doric columns until facilities at London Bridge were completed.

Throughout the 1830s, several companies were proceeding through Acts of Parliament to establish new routes. One company that had been quick off the mark was the London & Birmingham Railway (LBR), which took a bold approach and decided that it would locate a terminus in the Euston area of London, and another at Curzon Street in Birmingham, both of which were place in 1838. As had been the case in Liverpool, the limitations of the nascent locomotive designs in hauling loads over then insurmountable gradients influenced the company in their choice of a cable haulage system to draw trains from Euston to Camden where the gradient became acceptable.

The LBR dealt with this by locating the winding engines in cavernous, subterranean vaults, with a system of pulleys and counterweights powered by fixed steam engines. The only visible evidence of the location of the vaults at the time was the presence of two tall chimneys rising some 100ft (30m) above the track level, at the time a significant, and undoubtedly impressive, change to the local skyline. The vaults still exist, within which two winding engines were originally proposed, one for the L&BR and one for

the GWR, which initially was also intending to use Euston as its London terminus. The GWR engine was never used as the company abandoned its plan, instead locating its London terminus at Paddington.

The LBR (later becoming part of the London & North Western Railway (LNWR)) used the services of the eminent architect Philip Hardwick (1792–1870) who furnished the frontage of the large iron train shed at Euston, designed by engineer Francis Fox in 1837, with a large Doric portico to provide a grand gateway to the railway and to those arriving in London. Hardwick was later responsible for the classical, expansive space known as the Great Hall (1849) and replicated his classical theme of the Doric portico in the entrance building to the station at Curzon Street in Birmingham (1838).

Within a few years the rapid development of more efficient locomotives had made the need for the winding engines obsolete, and the ability to use a greater number of tracks to meet the increasing demand of passenger numbers meant that new terminal stations in London developed into grand cathedral-like structures, very much in the form that we see them today. The increased size was achieved due to the construction of imposing overall roofs, using new materials and design techniques. The stations were also invariably furnished with grandly styled frontage buildings, housing accommodation for passengers and staff and often also overnight accommodation.

The early design drawings for the railway are invariably exquisite works of art, usually highlighted by coloured aquatint and with exacting calligraphy. As this initial pioneering period was prior to the advent of photography, the works were generally illustrated in lithographs and it is very fortunate that the early projects of the railway companies were lavishly illustrated in contemporary engravings by John Cooke Bourne (1814–96), who produced magnificent illustrations of the key buildings and construction of the L&BR and the GWR.

Francis Thompson, architect for Robert Stephenson's North Midland Railway c.1840, commissioned illustrations such as this view of Derby Station from Samuel Russell, a contemporary of John Cooke Bourne and Thomas Talbot Bury (Midland Railway Study Centre, Derby, RFB28521).

Bourne's illustrations are generally in monochrome, although coloured examples do exist. However, there are superb examples of coloured illustrations of the stations and structures of the Liverpool and Manchester Railway, and the London & Greenwich Railway, produced by architectural detailer and illustrator Thomas Talbot Bury (1809–77), which were originally printed in London by R. Ackermann & Co., and are excellent references for understanding the nature and quality of the original designs.

John Dobson's original designs for Newcastle Central allied an imposing frontage building to elegant, arched train-shed roofs. Additional spans were constructed by William Bell for the North Eastern Railway (NER) in 1894. (Photo: Robert Thornton)

In the north-east, after the early building work by the Stockton & Darlington Railway (SDR), under George Stephenson, which had developed several buildings at the great locomotive building centre of Shildon, work moved apace. John Dobson (1787–1865), one of the most noted of northern architects, and who had been working on the redevelopment of the city of Newcastle, was engaged to work on designs for the Newcastle & Carlisle Railway (NCR) and developed the magnificent station at Newcastle Central, alongside Robert Stephenson in 1850, with its sweeping curved platforms and overall iron and glass roof.

Dobson's architectural work would later be expanded in 1863 with the addition of a large porte-cochère designed by Thomas Prosser, who himself worked on Durham Station in 1857 for the NER. Elsewhere, local stations appeared on various routes from Newcastle, with NCR resident engineer John Blackmore designing stations along the route from Newcastle to Berwick with architect Benjamin Green: Morpeth Station being one of his fine examples. In East Yorkshire, George Townsend Andrews was engaged to design stations for the York & North Midland Railway (YNMR) during 1846, with Cottingham, Beverley and Bridlington all reflecting the quality of his work.

The GWR, in developing its route during 1840, was working with its idiosyncratic broad track gauge of 7 feet and ¼ inch and as a company had, under its overall control, several distinct associated companies, which all appeared during the latter years of

The former Bristol and Exeter Railway headquarters building of 1852, with its distinctive Continental-style twin 'pepperpot' towers. (Photo: Robert Thornton)

Penkridge Station by Thomas Brassey (1837) is a simple building, which has a Continental quality and differs in style from his later goods shed at Coleham Yard, Shrewsbury. (Photo: Paul Childs)

the 1830s. During construction of the initial major route between London and Bristol, the board of the company had facilities located along the route. Initially, most of the buildings produced by the company from the drawing board of Brunel were of neo-Tudor or Gothic design, Italianate styling becoming more common later.

For many years they used the offices in the original station at Bristol Temple Meads as their headquarters. This is a Bath stone building in the gothic style designed by Brunel in 1840, facing onto Templegate and connected to the surviving original-timber, hammer-beam-roofed train shed. The Bristol & Exeter Railway (BER), a component company of the GWR, had its own headquarters constructed in 1852 in a fine separate office building designed by Bristol architect

S.C. Fripp (1812–82) in a contrasting style, located opposite the Brunel Station.

Although generally, most of the designers working during the 1840s and into the 1850s were focused on either neo-classical form or neo-Gothic detailing, there are examples that moved away from more complex architectural details. In the West Midlands area this is exemplified by the earlier work undertaken by Thomas Brassey (1807–70), contractor for the Grand Junction Railway (GJR), who, working alongside George and Robert Stephenson, produced a notably different style for the three stations constructed between Wolverhampton and Stafford in 1837.

Brassey became one of the most important and influential railway builders the world has ever seen,

Jacobean elegance from Sir Henry Hunt at Stoke on Trent for the NSR, 1848. (Photo: Malcolm Wood)

responsible for building much of the early railways in France, and eventually extending his work into South America. The sole GJR survivor, at Penkridge (1837) sits at the southern end of Brassey's impressive Penkridge Viaduct.

The simplicity of Brassey's work contrasts with that of Sir Henry Arthur Hunt (1810–99), architect to the North Staffordshire Railway (NSR), with his more extravagant 'Jacobethan' designs for the stations at Stoke on Trent (1848), Longport (1848) and Stone (1849). His layout for the station at Stoke on Trent resulted in the arrangement of a fine civic square, fronted by both the station and the North Staffordshire Hotel which reflected the style of the fine station frontage. Stone and Longport stations follow the same basic design styling as Stoke on Trent but in smaller form, whilst further south, the Trent Valley Railway Station at Atherstone, designed by John Livock (1814–83) in 1847, is not dissimilar to the approach of Hunt, but has a stronger Tudor feel owing to the use of plainer gable details.

The Era of the 'Railway Mania'

Once the pioneer railways had become established and the major centres of London, Birmingham, Manchester, Liverpool and Newcastle had been connected, access to the expanding network was rapidly perceived as being key to the success of many towns and their environs. The later 1840s subsequently heralded a period of explosive growth of the network, particularly between the many important textile and manufacturing centres in what became the northern industrial heartland.

The competition for towns to be included on the expanding system was intense, as many entrepreneurs saw the possibilities to capitalize on advantageous links to the market centres and coastal ports. One of those who saw the opportunity and was not afraid to embrace it was George Hudson (1800–1871), later known as 'The Railway King'. Hudson, who hailed from York, looked at the routes that would generate the most interest from towns and cities predominantly in the north and set about forming companies to promote the development of the routes. Quite often the towns were set against each other in a bid to get the best deal, and Hudson developed quite a reputation for his style of negotiation, not necessarily a positive one, illustrated by his eventual failure in business. The impact of his activities was, however, of major significance in the expansion of the national railway network and the nature of the growth generated the accepted term for this period

Stowmarket Station, which, together with the similar style of Needham Market Station, both by Frederick Barnes (1846), could be the home of landed gentry, such was the style adopted to express the local vernacular. (Photo: Malcolm Wood)

of 'Railway Mania'.

As a result of the rate of development, some railway companies became dependent on support and funding from communities keen to be linked to the new railway. One of the more extreme cases was at Stowmarket in Suffolk, where the town was keen to be no less well treated by the Ipswich & Bury Railway with the quality of its station than its neighbours. The company had engaged architect Frederick Barnes (1814–98) to design a series of stations in 1846, with Needham Market, Stowmarket and Thurston being the candidates.

The design adopted by Barnes was Jacobean in style in red brick with stone dressings, furnished with Dutch-styled gables. When it looked as though a watered-down version would be necessary at Stowmarket due to shortages in available funding, the town raised a loan to ensure that the station would have the same level of architectural quality as that proposed for Needham Market.

By the latter years of the 1840s, the requirements at stations were becoming far more consistent across many companies, although the design interpretations were often more varied. In time, as parcels traffic grew, many stations were furnished with a bespoke space to deal with this business, usually with a counter and storage area. It was not surprising that stations themselves were gradually developing into larger and larger structures.

Patronage and the Battle of Architectural Styles

At the outset of the 1850s, design consistency on railways continued to be based mainly on the adoption of the architectural style favoured by the principal engineers. However, the results were often a direct product of the skill of the architects and assistants employed to interpret the intentions of the railway companies and their paymasters. Local industrialists and landowners also continued to be very keen to set the architectural standard, often to ensure that the importance of the station and the locality was clearly demonstrated. There were also landowners, over whose land the railway would be routed, who demanded a greater standard of architectural detail and quality to maintain the pastoral idyll of their estates.

In Lincolnshire, the Earl of Yarborough, who was chairman of the MS&LR, insisted that Sheffield-based architects Weightman & Hadfield produce a very

Market Rasen Station. Part of the MS&LR station of 1848 designed by Sheffield architects Weightman & Hadfield. (Photo: Paul Childs)

Ridgmont station is a fine example of the cottage orné style of the Bedford Railway: half-timbered, with steeply pitched tiled roofs and distinctive chimneys. (Photo: Paul Childs)

specific neo-Jacobean style for the station proposed to serve his estate at Brocklesby in Lincolnshire in 1848.

John Grey Weightman (1801–72) and Matthew Ellison Hadfield (1812–85) appeared to have had a very busy year in 1848, completing designs at Market Rasen for the MSLR, and at the now-closed Louth Station for the East Lincolnshire Railway, both of which had a classical entrance porch. In 1849 they also completed the station at Saxilby, Lincolnshire, for the Great Northern & Great Eastern Railway Joint, a Tudor design in plain brickwork with tall chimneys, and steep-pitched gabled roofs.

A similar approach to consistency was taken by the Duke of Bedford, with the construction of a series of stations between Bletchley and Bedford in 1846 for the Bedford Railway (later LNWR). Four stations were designed at Fenny Stratford, Ridgmont, Woburn Sands and Millbrook, all in broadly similar style and in keeping with the rural style of the tied cottages on the Woburn estate, through which the line passed.

The palatial station at Huddersfield is a major feature of the grand civic space of St George's Square. (Photo: Paul Childs)

The solitary remaining gable end and fanlight of the former paired stations dating from 1863 at Buxton. (Photo: Malcolm Wood)

Another striking example of a patron's approach was that of the design of Huddersfield Station (1850: Huddersfield & Manchester Railway & Canal Co., which became the LNWR and Lancashire & Yorkshire Railway Joint) by the father and son team of J.P. Pritchett Snr and Jnr, who were already employed by Earl Fitzwilliam, a member of the Ramsden family, the local patron of the town. Accommodation for two railway companies at a common location was achieved by using a layout with a central, two-storey portico linked to rectangular fronted lodges at each extreme by a colonnaded link. The arrangement became the defining feature of the grand civic space of St George's Square.

Buxton was another location where two separate railway companies shared a site, albeit side by side. It was created, in 1863, by architect John Smith, who produced a pair of similar structures under the guidance of Sir Joseph Paxton (1803–65), designer of the Crystal Palace. Paxton was appointed to oversee the station works at the insistence of the Duke of Devonshire, who had engaged him to design the gardens at Chatsworth House. The influence of Paxton can be seen in the solitary surviving large glazed fanlight window.

The pace of development during the mid-Victorian period was no less rapid further north, and particularly in Scotland where routes from the south were being promoted in association with English

A fine perspective believed to date from the mid-1920s, created by Edwin Maxwell Fry and showing (left) the original Southampton Terminus Station of 1840 by Sir William Tite, and on the right the proposed extention to the former Imperial Hotel dating from the 1860s. (Drawing: Private collection)

An example of Sir William Tite's work north of the border at Lockerbie, introducing the local vernacular of crow-stepped gables. (Photo: Paul Childs)

companies. Generally, the eastern side of the country was centred on NER and Great Eastern Railway (GER) associations with the North British Railway (NBR). In the west, the CR forged a liaison with the LNWR, whilst the Glasgow & South Western Railway (GSWR) eventually joined forces with the Midland Railway (MR).

A striking example of the wider geographic influence at the time is that of prolific architect Sir William Tite (1798–1873), who designed stations in the early years of the industry in the south of England for the London & Southampton Railway (later part of London & South Western Railway (LSWR)), with particularly early examples at Winchester (1839), Micheldever (1841) and Eastleigh (1841). The style reflected classical forms bordering on Italianate, with slated, hipped roofs, resulting in stations designed in the form of large, urban-scale domestic villas.

In the late 1840s, Tite, by now engaged to design several stations in Scotland for the CR, made a significant impact just south of the border at Carlisle, where a joint development by the Lancaster & Carlisle Railway (LCR) and CR saw him design the new and impressive station at Carlisle Citadel (1847) in a style that others have termed 'Collegiate

Tudor'. Clearly popular with both companies, he had also previously designed stations at Penrith, Carnforth and Lancaster (all 1846) for the LCR in addition to the notable station at Perth for the CR. Perth demonstrated another impressive solution not dissimilar in style to Carlisle. Elsewhere, Tite recognized the local vernacular with the inclusion of crow-stepped gables, as demonstrated at Lockerbie (1847: CR).

Further Expansion of the Network

Between 1850 and 1870, station sites rapidly developed, often as a common suite of structures, linked to platforms with associated buildings. The increase in rail traffic and, particularly the rise of goods as a core business, resulted in a greater need for capacity and consequently a more complex local control of movements. A station master's house and, in some situations, workers cottages, were also likely to be provided. Water towers, water cranes and other outdoor equipment used for servicing locomotives were also a key feature of many station sites.

The Need for Operational Control Mechanisms

Prior to 1860, signalling on the railway was generally a case of individual manual control, often by dedicated railway 'policemen' housed in simple protective shelters. As routes multiplied and there was greater need for both directional and capacity control, it became necessary to develop a system of train controls that would be reliable, reduce the risk of human error and maintain safe separation between trains. John Saxby (1821–1913) was one of the first to look at protecting specific lines to prevent trains being on the same sections of track at the same time. They were to be controlled at points where directional divergence and convergence could occur.

The housing of the manual control mechanisms for the associated signalling systems and track operations were to create an entirely new building form in the shape of the signal box that we all know today. In pure elemental design terms, these are possibly the best-known and most iconic buildings specifically related to a railway function and, until the development of multi-functional control centres in more recent years,

they have a unique identity that is entirely derived from that function.

By the end of the second Railway Mania of the 1850s to 1870s the number of mechanical signal boxes had begun to rise at a high rate and it is recorded that as many as 10,000 signal boxes existed at the time of the 1948 nationalization. Most of these were from the Victorian era. As many as 500 of these were still operating well into the twenty-first century.

Unlike other railway buildings, signal boxes tended to be designed by the companies that made the operational frames and initially were identified by the company names rather than the railways that used them, although eventually they did become recognized by railway company type, as many companies built their own signalling works.

Engineering Challenges in the Early Years

As alluded to earlier in the book, beyond the need for appropriate functional buildings, the most significant issue determining the success and character of the railway system was that of surmounting the

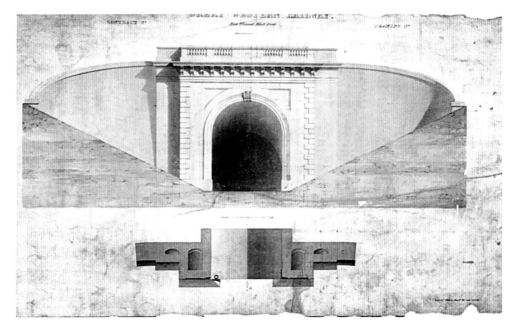

The western portal of Box Tunnel in Wiltshire, part of Brunel's GWR route to Bristol. (Drawing: Network Rail Archive)

Saxby, from Brighton, invented a mechanical interlocking system in 1856 which could control signals by means of cabling and rods, whilst also giving control of points at junctions to the signalman. The earliest signal boxes were simple cabins with half-glazed super-structures, carried on a framework of heavy oak posts. The signals were carried on tall posts formed as a continuation of the box itself, often with a timber-board walkway suspended at height between the signal posts. This was very precarious, as contemporary pictures show, and very soon the mechanical system of levers and interlocking mechanisms carried below a working floor within the box was developed, with the lower framework enclosed in lap boarding.

One of the oldest survivors of the second generation of signal boxes existed for many years at Billingshurst in Sussex. Known as a Saxby Type IB and dated from c.1865, it probably had been used elsewhere before being relocated to Billingshurst on the London, Brighton & South Coast Railway (LBSCR) where it was eventually fitted with a lever mechanism dating from 1877. A few years ago, improvements to signalling on the Arun Valley Line meant that the box became redundant, and it was relocated to a site at Amberley Chalk Pits Museum, where it remains as a fine example of a pioneer of what was to become the recognizable signal box which still exists on the railway to this day.

The 1866 Saxby 1B signal box, formerly located at Billingshurst Station, restored and resplendent at Amberley Museum. (Photo: Paul Childs)

challenges imposed by the topography and geography of the British Isles. The operational requirement for the track to be level, or as near level as possible, generated the need for the tunnels, embankments, bridges and viaducts that are so familiar now, and that have been accepted into the landscape. Landowners' concerns regarding the visual intrusion into their estates also forced some railway routes into cuttings and tunnels or wider diversions.

Architectural expression was not solely related to buildings but also to these engineering structures where they became visible. This led to some particularly elegant design solutions to tunnel portals and some subtle solutions to the issue of ventilating tunnels. In the case of the LBR, castellated round towers such as the Robert Stephenson example at Kilsby, Northamptonshire, were created to mask ventilating tunnels on the horizon.

The need for radical new engineering solutions produced some quite revolutionary-looking structures. Whilst it is now generally accepted that the best design solutions are those where form follows function in a simple manner, as for instance with Brunel's Maidenhead Bridge, the aesthetic

sensibilities of the mid-Victorian period often led to the inclusion of architectural details or flourishes that are now seen as forming an integral part of an engineering structure's character. This not only led to some very elegant classical solutions, as with David Mocatta's design for the Ouse Valley Viaduct on the London to Brighton line at Balcombe, but some inspired engineering designs such as the wrought-iron Conwy and Britannia tubular bridges in Gwynedd. Architectural input to engineering structures is exemplified by the entrance way to Liverpool Cemetery where the Bootle goods line passes the site and crosses the entrance. The cemetery was laid out in 1861 by Edward Kemp, an assistant to Joseph Paxton. Kemp engaged Liverpool architects Lucy & Littler to design the architectural elements to this unusual structure, including the portals to the bridge which are pure high Gothic.

Growth of Major Stations in the Capital

As previously observed, railways continued to expand at pace during the second half of the nineteenth

Anfield Cemetery Gates. High Gothic style for the Liverpool cemetery entrance, actually a bridge carrying the Bootle goods line. (Photo: Paul Childs)

The forecourt of King's Cross, Lewis Cubitt's masterpiece for the Great Northern Railway. One of a small number of Grade 1/A listed buildings on the rail network and fully restored in 2012. (Photo: Paul Childs)

century, and their terminal stations became grander and more opulent, reflecting the social and financial success of the enterprise.

London Paddington, which was originally constructed beneath Bishops Bridge Road, was replaced with a new station executed by Brunel in 1854. Working with Matthew Digby Wyatt, he produced the three-span station seen today, and this remained with little change until a fourth span was added in 1916. The terminus of the LNWR at Euston remained much as built in 1838 but with greater capacity achieved by extensions of the train shed, and a reconstruction of the entrance as The Great Hall in 1849. Euston was not then radically altered until the middle of the twentieth century.

St Pancras, with its 1868 train shed by Sir William Henry Barlow together with the hotel and entrance block by Sir George Gilbert Scott, was designed to make a statement on behalf of the Midland Railway, through the sheer scale of Barlow's single-spanned train-shed roof and the Gothic exuberance of Gilbert Scott's frontage building. The design of the station undercroft as a reception and storage point for one of the Midland Railway's key businesses, that of the transportation of beer to the capital, was based on the dimensions necessary for stacking the barrels. The design approach contrasted markedly with the style of King's Cross, its near neighbour. Constructed in 1852 to designs by Lewis Cubitt for the Great Northern Railway (GNR), the station was constructed out of necessity, as a result of impending structural failure of an earlier terminus station. Cubitt produced an elegant solution of paired train-shed spans, expressed at the front of the station by large semi-circular arched, glazed windows reflecting the form of the train shed behind.

Across the capital other terminal stations grew in importance and stature, most notably at London Bridge where the original London & Greenwich Railway station of 1836 was joined by structures for the South Eastern Railway (SER) and the LBSCR. The station teetered on the edge of barely adequate capacity and in 1866 was extended by the LBSCR with a large single-span arched structure, the work of H.E. Wallis and architect Charles Henry Driver, constructed over extra platforms to the south of the station. This would be the precursor to later major reconfigurations. As London Bridge was developed, Charing Cross (SER, 1864) and Cannon Street (SER: Sir John Hawkshaw, 1866) both became important terminals north of the river for the SER, developing a trend for commuter stations close to the City.

Consolidation from the 1860s

As the pioneering years and the energy of the Mania passed, the railway became a more stable entity, and architecture remained a key element in coping with the needs of an expanding system, not least in terms of passenger numbers. From the 1860s, basic railway station sites became even more expansive in terms of the commercial and operational functions requiring accommodation.

As railway companies merged or consolidated towards the second half of the nineteenth century, the emerging ancillary buildings reflected a trend towards greater standardization of style and detail, due in some part to the sheer volume of building material needed to deal with the increasing estate, and the need to employ trades well versed in their materials, able to work quickly and economically. The standardization of stations ran very much in parallel with the development of rolling stock and locomotive capabilities. Early rolling stock was initially based on four-wheeled carriages, but soon these extended to six-wheel vehicles and, later, to carriages with articulated bogies. This resulted in far longer trains, which in turn necessitated

longer platforms and this had an ongoing impact on the function of existing stations. This trend continues to this day as technology changes and demands on capacity continue to increase.

Goods Sheds Revolutionize Commercial Trade on the Railways

By 1870, most of the more significant station sites on most railways had a goods shed for trans-shipment or storage, often located just off the mainline, but adjacent to the station. Whilst the early sheds are usually small and often constructed of timber, the rapid development of the goods business soon forced many companies to consider not only the size of the sheds but also their location. Design decisions were based on the type of goods that were being transported, but also on whether the transfer of goods was from railway to railway where, for instance, the broad gauge met standard or narrow gauge, or where the transition was from railway to waterway or simply railway to road. The rare canal to rail trans-shipment and grain-storage shed at King's Cross is probably the best example of this type of building. Designed by Lewis Cubitt and completed in 1852 it dominates the surrounding yard and now forms the centrepiece of one of the most significant regeneration projects

The trans-shipment shed on the King's Cross Railway Lands is an outstanding example of the genre. Designed by Cubitt and built in 1852, it now forms the centrepiece of area regeneration and houses the relocated Central St Martins and public facilities. (Photo: Robert Thornton)

Wellingborough Station and goods shed are part of a suite of buildings designed by Charles Henry Driver with his favoured polychromatic brickwork for the Midland Railway. (Photo left: Railway Heritage Trust archive) (Photo below: Malcolm Wood)

in the UK.

The Midland Railway (MR), when opening a route from Leicester to Hitchin in 1857, appointed the engineering practice of Liddell & Gordon, and they employed architect Charles Henry Driver (1832–1900) to design a series of stations, notably at Hitchin, Kettering and Wellingborough. The latter is of particular interest, as Driver designed a suite of structures, all executed in a similar manner with regard to detail and materials. The station building itself was designed in what would become a typical style for the MR, incorporating two gabled pavilions linked by a recessed block, and reflected the need for increased waiting facilities.

The windows were of Gothic form, but a particular trademark of Driver was the use of black and white brickwork for the arches of window and door openings. He also introduced another typical MR feature in the use of cast-iron, lozenge-pattern window frames. Driver applied the same polychromatic brickwork detailing to the large goods shed located to the London side of the station building.

The shed also includes a series of three-centred arches (infilled in brick with lozenge-framed windows) and contains two gear-operated hoists fixed between the magnificent timber roof trusses and the timber platform. Not content with that, Driver also applied his polychromatic detailing to simple structures such a coal offices and weighbridge houses.

The GWR initially incorporated goods or parcel docks within the design of their overall train-shed stations, identifiable by three open bays as at the original surviving High Wycombe Station, but later constructed many simple goods sheds across their system during the 1850s and 1860s, initially serving broad-gauge rolling stock, but later incorporating transfer to standard gauge. The sheds were designed to be constructed in timber, brick or stone and incorporated the goods superintendent's accommodation as a small annex building constructed as a lean-to at one end of the structure, generally accessed from the goods-shed platform within the shed.

Demands of Locomotive Maintenance: Rise of Company Facilities

By the time of the Railway Mania the maintenance of locomotives had already begun to tax the minds of designers, and several examples of the locomotive roundhouse had been conceived and built. Locating a series of sheds around a turntable, or even a series of stabling sidings inside a circular plan-form shed became a workable solution to easy manipulation of locomotives for regular maintenance. Roundhouses existed at Chalk Farm on the LBR near Primrose Hill Tunnel, at Derby (MR) and at a smaller shed-based facility at St Blazey (Par), Cornwall (GWR). These structures were relatively industrial in form, but Chalk Farm Roundhouse is a fine, simple, circular brick structure with a conical slate roof and a magnificent trussed roof structure, now used as an entertainment venue. Derby's is now part of Derby College whilst St Blazey is a commercial venture.

The London & Greenwich Railway had been

erecting and maintaining rolling stock at Deptford from the late 1830s, working within the arches of the viaduct, but soon moved to bespoke facilities at New Cross. At Shildon in the north-east, the locomotive works had been established from the outset of the Stockton & Darlington Railway (SDR). The GWR established its works at Swindon in its early years, and the SER opened bespoke workshops for locomotive repairs at Ashford in 1847.

The exponential growth in buildings assets on the railway, particularly during the second half of the nineteenth century saw the development of design engineering teams capable of managing the design and construction of a wide range of building types. One only needs to look at the aerial photographs of locations, such as the Doncaster, York, Crewe and Swindon railway works, to see just how vast the building requirement of the main train companies were. Swindon is a particularly good example with the main locomotive and carriage works straddling the mainlines west from London and the domestic-scale housing, welfare and social facilities to the south of these works on the Swindon Old Town side of the line.

Companies began to seek locations where they could expand. The SER, having moved from New Cross in London to their new premises in Ashford in 1847, developed a wide range of facilities there. The design details were by Samuel Beazley, architect for Gravesend and Canterbury West stations, who was involved in designing various elements when the SER constructed a model village of housing, and social and community facilities at Ashford in 1851.

The Engagement of Architectural Resources

Adapting to the needs of the company boards appears to have been key in architects obtaining repeat business, sometimes in association with architects who might be regarded as rivals. NER, based in York, was unusual in that whereas most companies employed architects working under the chief engineer, the NER was prompt in setting up its own architect's

Leatherhead Station is attributed to Charles Henry Driver, architect for the LB&SCR. The roofing tiles are known as Taylor Patent Bridging tiles, designed by John Taylor who was architect for the L&SWR. (Photo: Malcolm Wood)

department. This followed the appointment of Thomas Prosser in 1854 who was appointed to a specific architectural post by T.E. Harrison, chief engineer. Later the architectural lead was positioned as a senior officer in the company, overseeing his own department. This situation continued right throughout the nineteenth and into the twentieth century, with one of the most influential personalities, William Bell (1844–1919), becoming company architect in 1877.

During Bell's tenure some important structures were created, including Tynemouth Station of 1882 and Darlington Bank Top of 1887, chiefly as a result of the prosperity of the NER.

In the south, between 1860 and 1890, the L&SWR was in full flow constructing stations along its main routes to the coast, as well as several branch lines, and the LBSCR continued to build apace, moving forward from the early designs such as the major terminus at Brighton designed by David Mocatta (1806–82) in 1841, where a new train shed was constructed at the rear of the original building, and the early, colonnaded frontage building became simplified.

A result of this general spate of expansion, the LSWR and the LBSCR began to develop stations with two of the original architectural sources, namely Sir William Tite and Charles Henry Driver. There appears to have been a bit of design crossover during the 1860s between John Taylor, architect for the London, Chatham & Dover Railway (LCDR) and the SER, and

Portsmouth & Southsea Station. One of several LBSCR stations based on details created by Charles Henry Driver. (Photo: Malcolm Wood)

A detail from Battersea Park Station that exemplifies two of the elements favoured by Charles Henry Driver: polychromatic brickwork and swirling filigree decoration. (Photo: Paul Childs)

Charles Henry Driver became a familiar name in the history of railway architecture starting with his original work for the Midland Railway. Other railway companies used him to design their stations, most notably the LBSCR, for whom he worked as a draughtsman under chief engineer R. Jacomb-Hood from 1865, with designs at London Bridge, Battersea Park and Peckham Rye stations.

When Joseph Bazalgette developed the London sewage system, Driver worked as his assistant between 1864 and 1866 and was a great exponent of the use of cast iron. This stemmed from his work on ventilation stacks or 'stink pipes', which were often immensely elaborate, and usually made by the Saracen foundry of Walter McFarlane in Glasgow. He was also engaged by Joseph

Paxton on designs related to the Crystal Palace. Driver is well known, too, for the magnificent interiors he produced for Abbey Mills and Crossness pumping stations. Later in his life, Driver designed several stations in South America, including the 'Station of Light' in São Paulo, and died a wealthy man in 1900.

Driver. John Taylor designed predominantly for the Kentish routes utilizing London stock bricks with red brick and faience highlight details and included cast-iron embellishments. He was noted for his patent design for clay 'bridging' roof tiles, which were used

on stations on the London, Chatham & Dover Railway (South Eastern & Chatham Railway), at Herne Hill Station (1862), Clapham High Street (1867) and Bat & Ball (1862: for Sevenoaks Railway, the station was originally called Sevenoaks). Driver, who was

One of the most iconic small stations in the Gothic style by William Tress for the SER, Battle Station opened in 1852 and reflects the details and materials of Battle Abbey. (Photo: Paul Childs)

responsible for Peckham Rye Station also used the Taylor bridging tiles there and at Leatherhead where Taylor and Driver's parent companies came together. Both architects favoured floriate stone string courses and applied cast-iron detailing.

The SER also used the design expertise of prolific architect William Tress. He was an exceptionally proficient exponent of the neo-Gothic style, as exemplified by his work at the magnificent little stations at Etchingham, Frant and, the most iconic of all, Battle. He incorporated lancet-style windows, tall chimneys with steeply pitched roofs and stone detailing, very

much in an ecclesiastical style, appropriate for its location. However, Tress was by no means solely an exponent of Gothic designs, as reflected in the station at Snodland in Kent, constructed in 1856. Adjacent to Snodland is Cuxton Station (SER: 1858), now sadly disused despite being part of the operational railway estate. Cuxton is a good example of the sparing application of a neo-Gothic style and exemplifies a marked contrast to its more classically detailed neighbour.

The inspiration of the Tudor period was also applied in the Eastern Counties and East Midlands area by Sancton Wood (1816–86) in his designs for

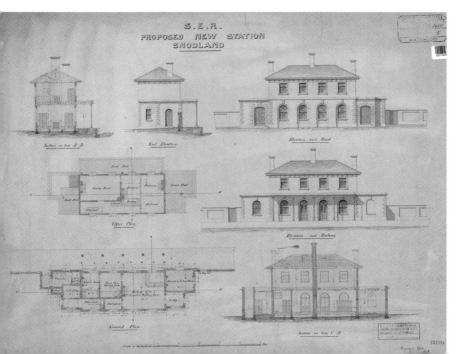

A fine example of a mid-nineteenth-century working drawing showing the proposals for the new SER station at Snodland located on the line between Strood and Maidstone in 1856. (Drawing: Network Rail archive)

Stamford Station, credited as a design from the pen of architect Sancton Wood, reflects the local style of the town of Stamford. The ashlar stone and Collyweston stone-slated roof lend gravitas to the image of the Syston & Peterborough Railway for whom it was built in 1848. (Photo: Paul Childs)

Stamford Station (1848) for the Syston & Peterborough Railway with an even more spectacular turret design than that used by Tress in the south-east. Wood used references to local styles from Stamford itself and stuck rigidly to the use of local ashlar limestone and Collyweston stone-slated roof detailing. There is also some thought that Wood was responsible, at least in part, for the design of Cambridge Station and the Ipswich and Bury Railway Station at Bury St Edmunds.

One of the most impressive stations in East Anglia is the distinctly Continental-styled station at Norwich Thorpe by W.N. Ashbee. Bearing similar features to the GWR station at Slough, it is another example of a form of French Renaissance design with curved pavilion roofs clad in fish-scale tiles, high ceilings in the interior and exquisite brickwork and fenestration.

The Midland Railway, having already used the services of C.H. Driver, began to adopt the basic pavilion form of Driver's designs. However, they did move away from this approach at times at the turn of the 1860s. The iconic station at Cromford was built in stages from 1855 to 1875, where accommodation was

Continental elegance exemplified at Cromford by the Midland Railway, 1855. (Photo: Malcolm Wood)

grouped in the cutting around a tunnel mouth, with a provincial French Renaissance approach exemplified in a turreted station master's house set high on the embankment face. This overlooked a small building housing platform accommodation in a similar style, complete with a chateau-style turret. The architect for the two early elements was G.H. Stokes (1826–71), son-in-law of Sir Joseph Paxton, the designer of the Crystal Palace. Paxton was a friend of George Stephenson and Thomas Brassey and a shareholder in and director of several railway companies.

The LNWR employed the skills of Francis Thompson (1808–95), the son of a builder from Woodbridge in Suffolk who had worked closely with engineer Robert Stephenson on the North Midlands Railway in 1840, with involvement in diverse schemes at Derby and Leeds, which included both station elements and sheds. The Midland Hotel Derby remains as an example of his work of this period. He also worked alongside Sancton Wood and Sir Henry Hunt on projects for the Eastern Counties Railway (ECR) in the late 1840s. Working for Stephenson in 1848, he developed an Italianate style for his magnificent station at Chester, for a L&NWR constituent company, the Chester & Holyhead Railway. He went on to be involved with the Britannia Bridge spanning the Menai Straits, and also to design the stations at Bangor, Bodorgan and Valley.

One of Francis Thompson's masterpieces in a familiar Italianate style. The long range of the station frontage was commissioned by the Chester & Holyhead Railway and opened in 1848. (Photo: Paul Childs)

Chapter Four

The Late Victorian and Edwardian Period – 1870–1922

Stable Growth

Between 1860 and 1870 most of the nascent railway companies had fully established themselves and the period saw a good few years of stable growth, but there were still many routes that had not been taken up.

The GWR was quick to absorb a lot of its constituent railways and, by the time of Brunel's death in 1859, the team of assistants that Brunel had put together began to be more instrumental in the development of new designs. One of the key players was William Lancaster Owen (1843–1911). He was the son of one of the original engineering assistants, William George Owen (1810–85), who had taken over the mantle of chief civil engineer after Brunel's death. In the west, the GWR was moving on from the Brunel era, and was busy building new station facilities at many locations to cope with an expanding customer demand and the development of goods and commercial services.

The architectural design responsibility in the 1870s was focused on W. Lancaster Owen and John Earley Danks. They designed a series of medium-sized stations that were constructed generally, but not exclusively, in red brick with blue brick quoins. The main

Dating from 1878, Torquay Station represents the Continental style adopted by W. Lancaster Owen and J. Earley Danks for medium-sized GWR stations in the 1870s. (Photo: Malcolm Wood)

feature of the stations was a frontage building with paired French-style truncated turrets in zinc or slate, topped by decorative wrought-iron crestings. The windows generally were of a sash form, but eventually became 'school board'-style windows, which had fan-lights of multi-pane glazing. One key feature was the development of standard platform canopies, which were a development necessitated by longer plat-forms. These were originally constructed of timber supported on cast-iron spandrels and columns, but eventually became far more functional in riveted iron and later riveted steel, representing a strong, early example of standardized design. The economies of procurement saw specific designs being utilized by many of the railway companies. Spandrels were generally decorated with swirling foliate designs, in direct contrast to the earlier simple Gothic-styled geometric piercings.

Great Malvern

One of the most iconic stations constructed during this period was the Gothic masterpiece at Great Malvern (1862), designed by noted local architect Edmund Wallace Elmslie (1818–89) for the Here-ford & Worcester Railway, a subsidiary of the GWR. Elmslie specialized in ecclesiastical architecture and local domestic villas. Using a random ragstone con-struction, Elmslie's stations at Great Malvern and Malvern Link reflect a crossover between the local vernacular and the railway. Great Malvern retains much of its original character, although the won-derful timber clock spire was removed and then part of the roof of the station was destroyed by a fire in the 1980s. The elegant porte-cochère has long gone. The lancet windows, steeply pitched gables and cast-iron crestings retain the original style, as do the stone details and the wonderful decorative column capitals on the platforms, portraying the flora of the Malvern Hills. These are attributed to

Originally built for the Hereford & Worcester Railway in 1862, one of the network's most iconic stations is Great Malvern, built in ragstone and with high levels of decorative detail. (Photo: Robert Thornton)

The longevity of Brunel's Italianate chalet design, which originated from the early 1840s, is exemplified by the recently restored stone 1873 example at Pantyffynnon on the Heart of Wales route. The reinstatement of the original style of dovecote chimneys is a fine detail. (Photo: Paul Childs)

William Forsyth (1834–1915). One surviving element of the station is the quaintly named 'Worm'. This is a former enclosed and semi-subterranean passageway linking the station to the former Imperial Hotel, now a school. Unused and unloved for many years, it still displays vestiges of its almost unique corrugated-iron roof, original cresting details and cast-iron glazing panels: on reflection, it is a hidden gem.

Wales

The railway in Wales in the mid-Victorian period consisted of four distinct elements.

South Wales and the Valleys were very much the preserve of the GWR and its subsidiary the South Wales Railway (SWR). Station designs were initially based on the well-used Brunel 'Chalet' design, which had been seen at Chepstow, Newport, Pantyffynnon and Bridgend. However, the Valleys were still developing as a result of the burgeoning mining industry and development would be influenced by the 'coal barons', most notably the Marquis of Bute, with the immense station at Pontypridd and the classic design of Cardiff

Bute Road (now closed) being prime examples.

North Wales was split between the Chester & Holyhead Railway and its overarching company, the LNWR, with both companies using the architectural skill of Francis Thompson. The north of Wales was also the base of the Snowdonia slate industry, and key features were the narrow-gauge industrial railways of the area, with the routes of the Ffestiniog Railway being the best known.

The north and south of Wales continue to be linked by two routes effectively running on a north–south axis. The westerly route, the Central Wales Line, predominantly relates to the LNWR, linking local centres on a route from Llanelli to Shrewsbury and on to Chester. The easterly route links Newport in Gwent through Abergavenny and Hereford and the marchland towns of Leominster and Ludlow to Shrewsbury and Crewe and on to Chester. This was a combined route basically represented by the GWR in the south and the LNWR north of Hereford.

The GWR stations generally followed company standard principles of design although Abergavenny was a distinctive stone structure in a simple villa style. Hereford Barrs Court was designed by

Thomas Mainwaring Penson (1817–64) in a baronial style, with a steeply pitched slate roof and red brickwork with Gothic-styled stone window details. This location was a transition between the GWR and LNWR operations.

The northern extent of the Central Wales Line is defined by stone buildings very much more in line with the style of the LNWR with good examples at Llandovery, Ruabon and Llandrindod Wells.

The Cambrian Railway stations were in the main domestic-styled buildings furnished with a distinct style of bold, medieval-styled timber canopy supports. These can be seen at Welshpool (where the station building is now remote from the railway), at Newtown, Machynlleth and also at Aberystwyth. The latter was redeveloped by the GWR in the 1920s and now has a neo-classical frontage typical of the early Art Deco period, whilst Machynlleth is a sturdy, confident rough-stone building with a steep, slated, gabled roof, now no longer in full railway use, but nonetheless a dominant feature in the landscape.

Further along the Cambrian coast, the stations are, in the main, a variety of quite uninspiring, if not plain structures, many of them only furnished with a station house or shelters.

The Settle and Carlisle Railway

One of the larger projects of this era was the Midland Railway's mammoth undertaking: constructing a line to link Leeds to Carlisle via Settle, on a route driven through the inhospitable terrain of what is now North Yorkshire and Cumbria. It was to run from Hellifield at the junction with the Kendal route through Settle, Ribblehead and Appleby to Carlisle, traversing some awkward valleys with structures such as the imposing Ribblehead viaduct and necessitating tunnels driven through the higher fells. This was intended as a route in competition with the L&NWR's route which ran along the west coast through Preston, Lancaster, Oxenholme and Penrith to Carlisle.

The company entrusted the engineering of the line to J.R. Crossley, who worked with architect John Holloway Sanders (1826–84). Sanders was responsible for developing a series of stations based on the domestic style that had been developed originally by C.H. Driver for stations on the Leicester to Hitchin route. These were refined into a suite of buildings of varying scale by Crossley and Sanders, and executed on stations in the Derbyshire coalfield, such as Shirebrook and Cresswell (both 1875). The buildings retained the gabled pavilions of the earlier designs and included the recessed waiting space and lozenge-glazed screens by metal-work specialists, Richards of Leicester. The buildings were constructed in local materials, generally stone, and were furnished with decorative pierced barge boards. Sanders was the architect responsible for the southern areas of the Midland Railway, alongside Charles Trubshaw (1841–1917), who was the architect for the northern area from 1864 to 1874, responsible for designs at Hellifield and Skipton. From 1874 until 1884, Sanders was given overall responsibility as the company architect for the Midland Railway, with Trubshaw taking over from 1884 until around 1906.

One of the most complete examples of the Settle and Carlisle stations is at Settle (1876), where a long-ranged station building with twin gabled pavilions is part of a larger site with workshops, a typical Midland Railway signal box and a water tower with masonry ground floor topped by a Braithwaite water tank. This particular structure has now been given a new lease of life by a sympathetic restoration and conversion into a residential property. The station at Garsdale (formerly known as Hawes Junction) also has a fine suite of structures, whilst at Dent there is a series of railway workers' cottages, which represent a rare survival on the route. These serve as a reminder of the vast number of workers who toiled in the worst of conditions to construct the line.

Settle Station is one of the largest examples of this Midland Railway style of station, part of the 1875 construction of the magnificent Settle and Carlisle route. (Photo: Paul Childs)

The Later Victorian Period 1870–1901

This period from 1870 to the end of Victoria's reign saw the infrastructure associated with railway operations grow to its largest and most complex extent. During this period many structures hastily built in the earlier era had to be rebuilt, for example Reading (1868 and later in 1899), although many of the smaller stations failed to reach this period due to the inadequacy and inflexibility of operational layouts. The key character of the stations and buildings of this period would eventually come to define the architectural character of geographical railway regions. Minor companies were slowly absorbed into the more dominant ones, as is later exemplified in the post-World War I Grouping, which, in effect, still contributes to the geography of the modern day routes and the associated operational and asset management.

The GWR and the Great Central Railway (GCR) both had interests in the route from north-west London through the Home Counties and on to Birmingham and Sheffield. The route from Paddington served the Thames and Cherwell Valleys through Oxford, Banbury, Leamington Spa, Dorridge and Solihull. The GCR ran through from Sheffield to the Midland Railway London terminus at St Pancras via Leicester, Loughborough and Bedford, but they had no link into Loughborough from the Chilterns area. The Great Western line serving the Chilterns originally ran from Maidenhead to High Wycombe, terminating in a Brunel train shed that still exists, albeit no longer in use. The line was later extended to Thame.

The GCR had the aspiration to open a terminus of their own in London, and to connect to their routes at Loughborough. The result of this was that the GCR

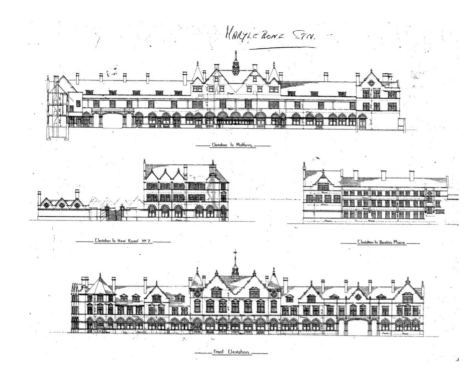

Elevation to Platform.

Elevation to New Road N° 7.

Elevation to Boston Place.

Front Elevation

Marylebone Station was built by the GCR in 1899 in red brick and buff terracotta. From being one of the capital's quietest terminals it now thrives as the main station on the Chiltern Railways route to Birmingham and is Grade II listed. (Drawing: Network Rail archive)

took a large parcel of residential land in the Marylebone area and, in 1899, set about constructing a fine terminus with a frontage building in Arts and Crafts style, fronted by a large glazed porte-cochère and a large hotel. There was also enough space to create a large goods station. The route out from Marylebone passed under the site of Lord's Cricket Ground by a long tunnel arrangement that crossed the LNWR route from Euston at South Hampstead. A joint line with the GWR was constructed from Marylebone to High Wycombe and beyond.

Architecturally, the stations developed at Gerrards Cross, Beaconsfield, High Wycombe, Princes Risborough and Bicester North all reflected the latest development of a GWR design, with the stations being designed in almost pattern-book form using red engineering brickwork with blue brick quoins and stone window-head details, allied to rivetted steel canopies that gave the stations a very solid, workmanlike feel.

The Edwardian Era and the Impact of World War I (1901–19)

The period immediately following the end of Victoria's reign heralded sweeping changes that were already underway both in modernization of stations and new design directions. Many stations, particularly in the south-west, were given extended platforms and individual canopies replaced overall train-shed roofs.

Charles Trubshaw, architect to the Midland Railway since 1884, spent some time in the late nineteenth century travelling in the United States. During his visit he became interested in the manner in which the American railroad companies dealt with the design of their more significant stations, and the distribution of passengers to the platforms. He returned to England with ideas for the necessary redevelopment of the stations at Leicester and Nottingham, using the notion of a distribution concourse spanning the tracks linked directly to the platforms by staircases. Access to the concourse from the road

This evocative view of Exeter St Davids from the early years of the twentieth century shows the transition from the former B&ER overall train-shed roof to the latest form of cantilevered canopies. Many older, larger stations were modified in this manner as the expanding railway demanded more, and longer, platforms. (Photo: Railway Heritage Trust archive)

was via an enclosed porte-cochère, which enabled transfer to and from road vehicles under cover.

Both stations were constructed on steel frames using detailing in locally sourced terracotta and faience and both were provided with extensively glazed roofs over their porte-cochères. They were also each furnished with eye-catching clock towers. The work at Nottingham was particularly notable for the bold detailing designed by local Nottingham architect Albert Edward Lambert (1869–1929), already noted for his work both in the city and on Nottingham Victoria Station. The style of his work was described in contemporary reports as English baroque. Leicester, on the other hand, included stylish graphics in an Art Nouveau style, with both stations containing elements of this genre.

Expansion of Rural Lines in Scotland

The period around 1900 also saw a trend towards the Arts and Crafts Movement. In Scotland, stations

Part of the 1903 reconstructions, along with Leicester and Sheffield stations, under the guidance of Midland Railway architect Charles Trubshaw, the faience and terracotta detailing of the Midland Station at Nottingham was produced by local architect Albert Edward Lambert. (Photo: Paul Childs)

Out in the wilds of the West Highland route, Corrour Station is over 10mi (16km) from a main road. The signal box was recently converted to provide holiday accommodation. It represents a fine example of the reuse of railway buildings, however remote. (Photo: Paul Childs)

on the West Highland Line followed the Arts and Crafts style and derivations of it also appeared on East Anglian routes such as at Ilford in Essex with red brick, stone details and clay-tiled hipped roofs. The reconstruction of Kettering by the Midland Railway under the guidance of Trubshaw was interpreted in faience and red brick, and, on the LBSCR, Bognor Regis (rebuilt in 1902 after a disastrous fire) Bexhill and Eridge stations also exemplified the style.

Whilst there had been rapid growth of the railway system in Scotland during the nineteenth century there was still a need for some communities to be linked into the main system and expansion of Glasgow and Edinburgh led to proposals for improved urban systems, allied to expansions of the main stations at Glasgow Central and Edinburgh Waverley. This was matched by a need for stations to be built that would be economic but robust.

The period at the end of the nineteenth century up to World War I saw a spate of construction by the

Designed by James Miller for the Cathcart District Railway, Maxwell Park (1894) is one of the ten stations executed in similar Arts and Crafts style on the Cathcart Circle in Glasgow. (Photo: Paul Childs)

railway companies of Scotland. Routes were pushed into remoter areas by the CR and the component companies of the Highland Railway. The West Highland Railway (North British Railway) and its extension of 1894 and 1901 respectively saw the introduction of a series of low-hipped roof-chalet designs, which were quite appropriate to their surroundings. Those at Rannoch and Tyndrum Upper and the stylistically different Corrour were particularly remote.

The CR and Glasgow & South Western Railway developed stations at West Kilbride, Prestwick Town, and Troon on the West Highland Railway route from Glasgow to Fort William (through 1894). They also developed stations on Glasgow's Cathcart Circle, using the consummate design skills of James Miller (1860–1947), who designed the Turnberry Hotel. At the same time, the eastern side of Scotland was being attended to with designs by NER architect William Bell for some medium to small, but nonetheless, significant buildings.

The Impact of World War I

World War I had major implications for the national railway system. The 123 companies were all involved with nationally significant logistical work, moving supplies, munitions and men. Many of the companies supplied men to serve in the armed forces, and many of those who went either never returned or were unable to continue in railway work. The sacrifice of the staff of the railway companies cannot be underestimated, and many fine memorials at stations are testament to their memory.

A major advance in transport resulted from World War I, in that, as the conflict progressed, road motor transport developed and driving skills were acquired. This meant that the flexibility of transport and the freedom it gave began to put a strain on the railway companies. There were also the privations of the post-conflict depression to contend with, but the national economy still needed to be serviced. This heralded the commencement of a drive to maintain the position of the railways in goods distribution, which would have major bearing on the future of the railways within a few years of the Armistice.

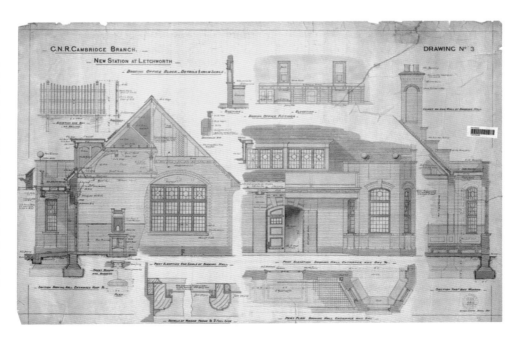

With the influence of the Ebenezeer Howard-inspired garden city at Letchworth, it was inevitable that the station would take on the styling of the Arts and Crafts Movement for which the town is known. Built by the GNR only one year before the advent of war in 1914, it is Grade II listed. (Drawing: Network Rail archive)

Chapter Five

Grouping and 'The Big Four' – 1923–47

Architectural Outlook

This period is characterized and wholly influenced by the two world wars that, in effect, 'bookended' it. As the impact of World War I leads to the formation of a completely new managerial structure for the entire railway network, so too does the impact of World War II and its aftermath only twenty-seven years later: a relatively short time in the overall history of the railways.

Whilst there was a later flurry of activity and some significant operational and building portfolio developments, the railway system as a whole was probably at its maximum scale of national coverage prior to 1914. The subsequent rationalizations of the system after the 1923 Grouping saw station closures and changes of operating methodology well in advance of the notorious and severe cuts of the 1960s. There was

The Victory Arch at Waterloo Station was designed as part of the main suite of offices by L&SWR architect J. Robb Scott. It was completed in 1922 as the main pedestrian entrance into the station and the memorial to those men of the company who died in World War I. The sculptures either side of the entrance represent War and Peace, and the whole is topped by a sculpture of Britannia. (Drawing: Network Rail Archive)

certainly no significant growth overall and this is why such a significant proportion of today's underlying main-line infrastructure is Victorian.

With only one or two exceptions, this period didn't produce any startling architectural methodologies or indeed architecture in respect of the railway context, despite often being regarded as a golden age of rail travel. It was perhaps not as architecturally innovative as would appear from the railway company publicity and promotional campaigns, the posters for which in themselves are of the highest quality. It is entirely possible when looking at this material from a twenty-first century perspective that we overlook what the everyday travelling conditions were like for passengers. What the posters depicted was very much leisure travel. Those produced for the London & North Eastern Railway (LNER) by the likes of Tom Purvis, Frank Newbold and Fred Taylor, where the subject matter is often of golfers and grand hotels are great examples of commercial art in the railway context of this era. Even the great industrial heartlands of the country were romanticized in the paintings of Norman Wilkinson RA for the London, Midland and Scottish Railway (LMS).

Each of the railway companies embarked on premises redevelopment proposals during this period but the truly adventurous projects, such as the proposals to rebuild the major termini, mostly foundered as a result of the threat of war. Some of these were resurrected in the period immediately after World War II but came to nothing as the new era commenced.

It is rather telling that the birth of this period started with the completion of the Victory Arch at Waterloo Station that had just seen the engraving of those railwaymen lost in World War I and it ends with the design and construction of buildings designed to withstand the onslaught of another conflict, and that had been adapted to include the many war memorials that had been dedicated to the railwaymen and women that had lost their lives in the earlier war.

Amalgamation

The 123 railway companies that remained in existence at the close of World War I had suffered severe losses and following a review of the contribution that they made to the economy the government enacted the Railways Act of 1921 in the national interest. The key consequence of the Act was the amalgamation of many companies and the formation of the four major companies under what was to be termed 'Grouping': the GWR, the London Midland & Scottish Railway (LMS), the LNER and the Southern Railway (SR). These companies became known as the 'Big Four'.

Most of the railways of Wales went to the GWR, which already was the sole operator for much of the route to the south-west, which it would cover under Grouping. The LMS took over the Midland Railway, the Lancashire & Yorkshire Railway and the LNWR, together with some companies in Scotland. The LNER took over the NER, the Great Northern Railway and the remaining companies in Scotland. The SR encompassed the LSWR, the LBSCR and the South Eastern & Chatham Railway (SECR).

It is known that the architect's departments that were created out of the amalgamation were under the jurisdiction of the chief civil engineers for each company, but their precise location is not clear, although it is likely that they would have been co-located in the headquarter offices of each new company. The heads of the architectural teams in each group would have been known as chief assistants and under this reorganization a prominent name becomes associated with each office for this relatively short period, for instance, J. Robb Scott on the SR, Percy Culverhouse on the GWR and William Hamlyn on the LMS.

All four of the new companies inherited distinctly different commercial backgrounds, both in terms of the business images of their constituent railways, but also in the manner with which design, particularly that related to buildings, had been managed. The GWR found itself in the most settled of positions. It had continuing control of routes that it knew well, and it had already embarked on a programme of

Opened in 1926, Margate spans the transition from the Arts and Crafts-flavoured Beaux Arts styling of the Edwardian period and the emerging modern influences of the 1920s. The restoration of the 2010s enables it to be seen as originally intended. (Drawing: Network Rail archive)

development in the final years of the nineteenth century and leading up to World War I.

Whether it was to alleviate the experience of the carnage of the war or the dark era that followed, there was certainly a shift of architectural mood to looking forward stylistically rather than backward. There was also a recognition by central government that it needed

to maintain a good railway system in the national interest. By this period, the railway system as it had become known was nearly a hundred years old and needed further investment for essential maintenance and also expansion. This fact together with the government's perceived need to assist employment in the country led them to passing the Development (Loan Guarantees

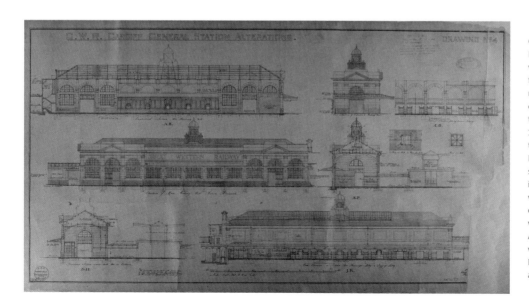

GWR architect P.E. Culverhouse was responsible for much of the reconstruction of stations on the GWR in the 1930s including the now Grade II listed, main station building in Cardiff, which was constructed of Portland stone with a number of Art Deco features within. (Drawing: Network Rail archive)

Surbiton is the most thoroughly worked of the 1930s SR stations with substantial buildings on the up and down sides. The entrance areas in both buildings provide memorably lofty spaces, unusual in a suburban station. (Photo: Paul Childs)

and Grants) Act of 1929, which provided funding for improvements related to the freeing up of bottlenecks and enhancing capacity, particularly at 'through' stations. Funding under this initiative was consequently provided at major rail centres, noticeably on the GWR at such stations as Bristol Temple Meads and Paddington as well as strategically important regional centres such as Newton Abbot, Newport and Cardiff and later at Leamington Spa. The LMS and the SR also recognized the need for modernization, with the LNER following suit with its own plans.

Architectural Aspirations

The style of the architecture selected for building projects in the 1930s was often pattern-book Edwardian, but a new style also emerged, now loosely (and generally in this text) called 'Art Deco' but sometimes referred to as 'Moderne' at the time. The influences that engendered the change in direction of the railway architects was encompassed in the ethos of the 'Roaring Twenties' and the 'Jazz Age'.

Away from the railways there was a quest for speed, based on the developments of vehicles and aircraft, and the greater affinity with the internal combustion engine. This was based on the knowledge and experience of many coming back from the war with their increasing contact with a rapidly changing, mechanized world. The quest for speed was also prevalent on the railway with developments in efficient steam engines and the use of streamlining. This aspiration manifested itself in the approach to the design of buildings and found expression by the use of horizontal emphasis, particularly in window proportions and framework design, and the use of curved brickwork as in the SR signal-box designs at Woking and Templecombe.

There was certainly competition between the companies to sell their services on the basis of speed, and expressive architecture was well at the forefront of this campaign. As with society, design became more fluid and liberal with the constraints of the classical orders being set aside to allow the development of new forms.

The SR were, in a way, pacesetters for the changes to the railway architectural portfolio. Influences from the United States that had been initially lauded by Trubshaw for the Midland Railway now engaged the minds of J. Robb Scott, architect for the Southern Railway, and his assistant, Edwin Maxwell Fry who appears to have been inspired by the station design for Yonkers in New York in his design for Margate. Ramsgate, designed at the same time, reflected a more reserved but distinctly English Art Deco style. Hastings also followed these stylistically but was demolished in 2004 to make way for a new station building by Howard Fairburn MHK.

One of the key drivers for the SR was the widespread development of the electrified railway and the crisp graphics that the SR included in their signage, thus reinforcing futuristic aspirations. Architecturally, this manifested itself in the development of an International or Moderne style for the stations at Woking and Surbiton on the south-west mainline from Waterloo towards Southampton. At Southampton itself, the station serving the transatlantic liner port was restyled in a brash style full of details referencing the magic of the great liners. Prominent in this style were the outer suburban stations of Tolworth, Haywards Heath and New Malden but perhaps the best and most complete of these as a station is Surbiton with its dominant lift towers driven by the inclusion of a significant parcels' handling operation.

The SR did not just rest with the stations, but also developed a stylish series of Art Deco signal boxes and electrification control centres with curved corners to the buildings and canopies, appropriate metal-framed windows, and brick and concrete construction. Again, 'super-graphic' signing was a paramount detail.

The LMS were no less bold, although their introduction of Art Deco was on a smaller number of stations and buildings such as Leeds north concourse, and the remodelling of the linked Queens Hotel. Of the smaller stations, Hoylake stands out but perhaps the most iconic structure of the era in the LMS portfolio was their hotel at Morecambe designed by architect Oliver Hill, with additional details by renowned designer Eric Gill. Whilst these might be overtly Art Deco, the chief architect of the LMS, Hamlyn, also designed buildings in a classical style with Art Deco flourishes. Not wildly lauded by critics to date, these are nonetheless robust buildings with interesting details and can be seen at the former Staff Management School at Derby and the former headquarters building for the LMS in Eversholt Street in London.

Also by Hamlyn, one of the more curious buildings of this period and perhaps not given a second glance by its users is the brick-built Luton Station which has a twentieth-century Scandinavian feel to it.

The use of faience tiles, glazed bricks, steel windows and flat roofs characterized the GWR's interpretation of this style whereas on the SR and LMS, a mixture of brick, concrete and painted render were to dominate. Curved surfaces and flat roofs came to characterize the new SR stations, signal boxes and electrical sub-stations that were to support the wholesale DC electrification of the region.

In respect of the GWR it is probably not clear until the 1923 Grouping how architectural resources were allocated, but certainly a figurehead in the form of Percy Emerson Culverhouse emerged and his team's influence is still visible at stations such as Paddington (former Arrivals Side offices), Cardiff, Bristol Temple Meads and Leamington Spa.

There were many commercial railway property proposals and also hotel extension proposals during this period. As the railway companies looked forward, they also saw the need to demolish what we would now regard as sacrosanct buildings. Even whilst acknowledging their importance, the board of the GWR put forward plans to expand Paddington Station in its entirety and replace the wrought-iron Brunel structures with reinforced concrete, albeit in barrel-vault fashion. Similar plans for the rebuilding of Euston Station were commissioned by the LMS and likewise King's Cross for the LNER. Whether any of these were genuinely feasible in straitened times is debatable but they illustrate clearly what the mood of the times was and how little the past was regarded when planning for the future.

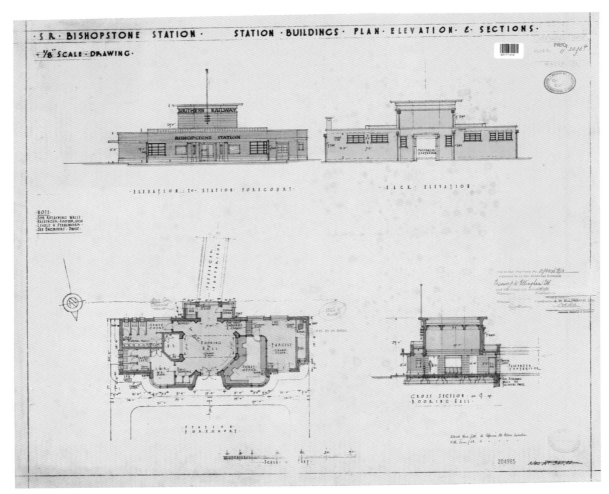

James Robb Scott, architect of the SR, was a strong advocate of Art Deco, such as the 1938 design for the small coastal station at Bishopstone in Sussex. At the outbreak of World War II, the roof was cleverly modified with two machine-gun positions either side of the central drum. (Drawing: Network Rail archive)

World War II Intervenes

Railway companies were quick to focus on the security of their structures in anticipation of hostilities in the late 1930s. The LMS paid heed to the impending crisis by designing a signal box that could be located at critical points on the system. With a concrete frame and bombproof entrances, the best surviving example is that located at Runcorn in Cheshire. The SR modified their 1938 Art Deco station at Bishopstone on the Sussex coast with additional machine-gun ports on the roof either side of the central drum.

Where in-house architects were busy on a daily basis providing most of the construction requirements of the industry throughout the twentieth century, they could not necessarily turn their hand to major commercial redevelopments of the sort that the Big Four wished to explore between the two world wars. The major plans for the wholesale rebuilding of Euston and Paddington, the first by Sir Percy Thomas and Partners and the second by Henry Tanner and Partners, are typical examples of these. It would have been difficult to divert in-house resources at this stage so presumably these external resources were taken on to supplement skills in new or unfamiliar areas or to avoid conflict with core operational work. It is not known whether they were in any way managed by or consulted with the company architects.

Many of these plans were put on hold when World War II became inevitable and, whilst there was a little resurgence of in-house activity on the design front immediately after 1945, the recovery and the dawning of the nationalized era in 1947 reappraised those plans, many of which were consequently dropped in favour of a collective industry modernization programme.

The government-appointed Railway Executive Committee controlled the railway operations of the Big Four for the duration of World War II, which wore out every part of the railway infrastructure. Not only did much bomb damage have to be repaired after the conflict but much deferred maintenance had to take place across the entire country. In the aftermath of war, this could only be done on a funds-permitting, ad hoc basis.

Seeing a further need for government intervention in the future of the railway as being in the national interest, the government of the day passed the 1947 Transport Act, which came into effect on 1st January 1948. This enactment created The British Transport Commission (BTC) under whose umbrella came waterways, docks, rail and road transport.

Even between the conclusion of war activities and the nationalization itself, the railway companies put forward proposals for restored and improved services and facilities. The LNER, for instance, suggested that in addition to the repair of depots, yards and track damaged during the war, new station facilities should be built at King's Cross, Peterborough, Grimsby, Middlesborough, Leeds and Glasgow Queen Street. Over 300 stations were to be repainted and, in all, the estimated cost amounted to more than £50 million. How much of this proposal, and those formulated by the other railway companies, transferred into the nationalized era and in what timescale is not clear.

The redevelopment proposals for Paddington, dated 1922, included a new expanded structure for the station and a combination of major office expansion and commercial development to assist funding it all. The architects Henry Tanner and Partners were appointed for this aspect. (Drawing: Network Rail archive)

Chapter Six

The Nationalized Period – 1947–94

Overview of the Period

The nationalized period takes one from the beginning of 1948 through to 1994/7 commencing with the reassembly, repair and modernization of a railway system that had suffered greatly during World War II. Overall, the period was significantly affected by three key economically driven moods and changes in management direction, all of which resulted in major changes for the structure of the industry and, ultimately, changes in the responsibilities of the company and consultancy architectural teams and the work they did within the industry. The 1950s was characterized by modernization – and, perhaps, optimism in respect of architecture; the 1960s and 1970s by reshaping, and the 1980s and 1990s by a change from a functionally led to a business-led railway (known as sectorization), leading the way to privatization.

Whilst this period started with an optimistic, but maybe misjudged, approach to modernization, it

PLYMOUTH STATION RECONSTRUCTION

British Rail Western Region's proposals for the comprehensive rebuilding of Plymouth Station, embracing offices, signal box and new station, typifies the optimistic approach to architecture during the 1950s. (Image: Railway Heritage Trust Archive)

eventually saw a more rapid rate of change to the infrastructure it inherited than any equivalent period prior to it, this time not in terms of growth but in shrinkage. With the notoriety it has now built up, some observers have viewed this period as the third Railway Mania. The period, spanning nearly fifty years, also saw many architectural fashions that are, perhaps, not fully assessed or articulated as yet.

The initial architectural optimism that saw the design of, say, Coventry Station and the Rail Technical Centre in Derby made way for a period of cutbacks and recession towards the end of the 'Swinging Sixties' and into the early 1970s. However, the introduction of high-speed trains in the mid-1970s lifted the mood and the targeted investment in a number of station developments heralded a new era for railway architecture as the eighties approached under new chairmanship that also saw renewed interest in the heritage and the potential it had to enhance the quality of service for rail passengers.

Each of these phases had consequences for the future and design of operational buildings, not least of which was the impact of many of them becoming operationally redundant following the major reduction in the scale of the system in the 1960s.

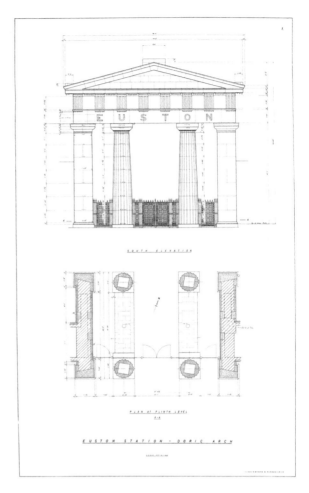

One of BR (LM) Regional Civil Engineer's survey drawings of the Euston Arch prepared in advance of the demolition of the structure and after the consideration of a relocation to the south-east corner of Euston Square. Its destruction affected all architectural criticism of the later nationalized period. (Drawing: Midland Railway Study Centre)

The Challenge of Change

During this period, the management of the operational buildings portfolio and the engagement of appropriate design professionals changed greatly. First, it saw the development of in-house architectural practice resources up to the mid-1980s. Then came the change in emphasis to the greater engagement of consultants and the consequential need for these resources to become professional 'buyers' of services and the setters of appropriate design standards for adoption by contracted consultancy services.

To put into scale the impact of the changes that took place to the infrastructure over the duration of this period it should be noted that the combined railway companies at the outset of nationalization in 1948 comprised more than 600,000 men and women operating 20,000 route miles of track, connecting approximately 7,000 passenger and goods stations. At this time the railway industry also ran 11,000 motor vehicles for onward dispatch of goods, and, still at this time, 25,000 horse-drawn delivery vehicles for goods and parcels, requiring 7,000 horses, all of whom had to be stabled, fed and cared for in specially designed premises. There were also 70 steamers on Continental and Irish services belonging to the train companies.

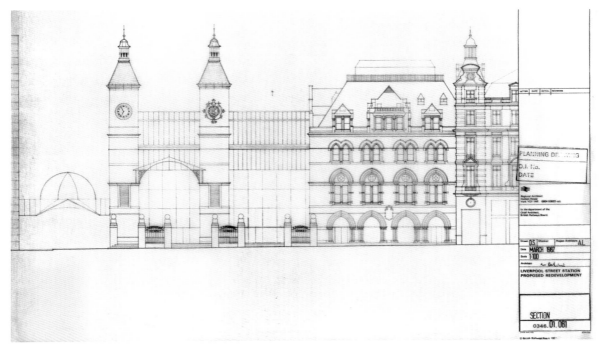

One of the many hundreds of traditional design drawings by British Rail's Architecture and Design Group of the Liverpool Street new entrance to the station and 50 Liverpool Street, which was to be a complete reconstruction. (Drawing: Network Rail archive)

These statistics would look very different by the end of the period when there were fewer than 150,000 staff in BR and fewer than 2,500 passenger stations. The docks and ferry services together with the hotels and engineering works had been sold off and there were no horses! These reductions were not the only changes requiring different building needs: the change from steam-power traction to diesel and electric, the change from wagon-load freight to train-load freight, the loss of parcels and mail traffic and the massive reduction in the workforce and so on, all placed different building needs on the industry. These statistics and the regular changes to them had a significant bearing on the architectural resources that the train companies needed to engage with.

In addition to the concerns raised by the major changes to the system and the impact on its architecture, this period also witnessed the most notorious and perhaps the most significant events in respect of future views on architecture within the railway and beyond: namely, the threat to demolish St Pancras and

the actual destruction of the Euston Arch standing as the gateway to Euston Station. Whilst the cutbacks to the system emanating from the implementation of Dr Beeching's report will always dominate headlines, the impact of the demolition of the Arch has undoubtedly influenced railway architectural conservation thinking from that moment on.

Projects

The range and diversity of projects undertaken, planned or contemplated in this period is broad and perhaps it should be noted that some of those that will see completion and credit in the next period had their genesis in this era. This is particularly true of those connected with the consequences of the Cross London Rail study of 1989, such as Crossrail, the stations for which are now completed but awaiting operational introduction and Thameslink, the stations for which, such as Blackfriars, London Bridge and

Farringdon, have been rebuilt or extensively modified and are now open for business.

The many changes that occurred during the remainder of this period saw the completion of what may be considered to be its most significant architecture, the rebuilding of Liverpool Street Station and the building of the first international rail terminal at Waterloo. It also saw the birth of what became the most significant project to date in the privatized period, for instance, the creation of the second international terminal at St Pancras and its total restoration, which had been unthinkable only twenty-five years before. Whilst the station was completed in 2009, the development of its hinterland is ongoing.

It is perhaps interesting to note that the period saw a significant change in the process of architectural design. At the outset designs were produced by architects standing up at drawing boards with pens and pencils. By the late 1980s and early 1990s this methodology had given way to Computer Aided Design (CAD) with the reconstruction of Liverpool Street Station being one of the last of the big BR projects substantially completed in the traditional way.

Nationalization and Railway Architecture

The organizational structure of the nationalized industry broadly followed that adopted in the post-1922 Grouping period insofar as the continu- ation of the regions was concerned. However, it created a central command structure – the British Transport Commission (BTC) – to which the executives, of which there were five, were responsible. Each of the former Big Four became British Railways regions with two of them splitting their resources. The LMS became the London Midland Region and the Scottish Region: the GWR became the Western Region; the LNER became the Eastern Region and the North Eastern Region; and the SR became the Southern Region. Each of these newly titled regions had their own architectural teams working within civil engineering departments.

In acknowledgement, at a senior level in the industry, that railway architecture had not been sufficiently appreciated as an important genre to date, and that design would play a major part of the modernization programme envisaged at that time, the newly formed BTC created a new figurehead role for architectural design via a new chief architect's post. This person would lead and inspire the design direction of the amalgamated groups within the Commission. Dr F.F.C. Curtis Ing FRIBA, formerly the chief architect to the Great Western, was appointed to this role to herald a new, corporate era. However, the architects employed in the newly formed organization under regional civil engineering departments were not directly responsible to him.

The newly created chief architect had his own office located in Marylebone station, which generally

Dr Frederick Francis Charles Curtis Ing FRIBA

The railway industry's first chief architect, Dr F.F.C. Curtis, had immigrated from Germany in the 1930s at the time of the Nazi rise to power and briefly worked for Charles Holden on the SR before teaching architecture at Liverpool University. He was appointed to follow Brian Lewis as the regional architect for the GWR in 1947 just prior to nationalization and in his short time there he completed the stations started by Lewis at Hanger Lane, West Acton, Greenford, South Ruislip and Perivale prior to his appointment as chief architect to the BTC in 1948, a role he carried through to 1968. Perhaps his most significant legacy is the design for the Railway Technical Centre in Derby, which with its clean modern lines, planning and landscaping earned a Civic Trust Award in 1969.

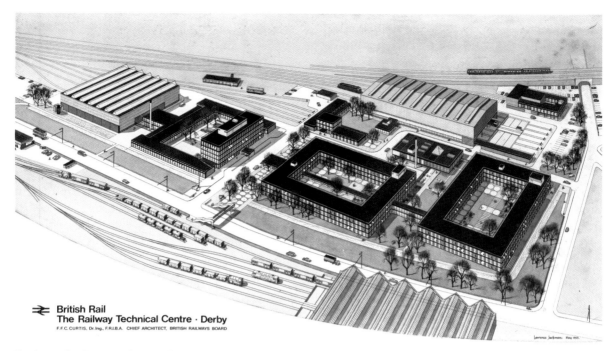

The former Rail Technical Centre at Derby was better known as the location of the development of the Advanced Passenger and High Speed trains, but the administrative offices are worthy of architectural note. Designed by the chief architect at British Rail and opened by HRH Prince Philip in 1964, it was bestowed with a Civic Trust Award in 1969. (Image: Private collection)

concerned itself with non-regional work such as hotels, administrative buildings, some station work and, most notably its single biggest work, the Railway Technical Centre (RTC) in Derby. This office later went on to design a diverse variety of projects including the hoverport at Dover, the British Transport Police College at Tadworth and the National Railway Museum at York. It also later secured the contract to design the stations on the Hong Kong/Kowloon railway via BR's international project arm, Transmark.

The mid-1970s saw the transfer of in-house professional architects within BR regional engineers' departments into a single autonomous entity. Support staff, such as building services engineers, clerks of works and quantity surveyors, were also more fully integrated. The 1980s saw the integration of the industrial design and graphics teams, and landscape architects. Collectively, these would then refocus their activities towards the BR sector-led business in the late 1980s and finally split into either a practice group or a design management group in readiness for privatization. In

recognition of the broader span of responsibility, the title 'Chief Architect' was replaced by the title 'Director of Architecture and Design' (DAD) and later to 'Director of Architecture, Design and Environment' (DADE). The central role forged by Dr Curtis as chief architect transferred first to Bernard Kaukus and then to Roy Moorcroft before the amalgamation of all design disciplines into the group. Bernard Kaukas became the first Director of Architecture, Design and Environment and Jane Priestman followed into this role (1986–91), having been appointed from the private sector.

As the industry prepared for privatization, the architects and support teams grouped into a potential private practice or prepared to follow opportunities in the new railway companies.

Rebuilding the Infrastructure

The need to renew, replace or rebuild a number of smaller stations as part of the modernization programme at the outset of the period led to the search for appropriate standardized or, indeed, modular solutions. Each of the newly formed regions explored ways to do this, taking into account post-war austerity. Whilst this approach was appropriate after the war, research into such methodology had, in fact, been undertaken in the 1930s to establish an economic way to replace ageing buildings, with the LMS architects at the forefront of this.

BR (LM) retained the services of Hamlyn as the former chief architect of the LMS after nationalization. One of his first tasks was to establish the optimum method for quickly rebuilding damaged and life-expired stations. Research into aspects of durability and flexibility of planning led to a steel-frame building clad with vitreous enamelled panels and precast concrete panels below windowsill height. The modular units were designed to utilize surplus materials from the war effort and the output of the LMS concrete depot at Newton Heath. The pioneer station for this methodology was Marsh Lane and Strand Road near Liverpool: others were built at Queens Park and West Hampstead, although the latter has now been removed.

A later programme of prefabrication was implemented on the Cheshire electrified lines at stations such as Hartford and Styall. These were of exemplary design principles in respect of proportion and detailing based around a prefabricated steel frame. Unfortunately, and as with other forms of simple and elegant design, this made them very vulnerable to the detractive impact of subsequent modifications, additions or applications of essential but often unco-ordinated station paraphernalia, such as posters and vending machines but, in particular, surface-mounted utility services and conduits, and so on. Some of those that still exist, as at Goostrey, have been altered beyond all recognition.

The Western Region experimented with propri-etary timber-framed buildings from the Vic Hallam Company but also devised its own rationalized trad-ditional (RAT-TRAD) small structures, affection-ately known as 'cattle-pen' structures after their first deployment on the former cattle-pen site at Reading station. The title was possibly regarded as an appropriate name by later critics of the system! The Western Region also produced a number of tim-ber-framed signal boxes on a modular plan although

This small waiting shelter at Goostrey typifies the application of the LM design principles developed during the 1950s. Examples that still exist are unrecognizable as the original elegant forms and whilst the substructure was retained at Goostrey, it has been very crudely reconfigured. (Photo: Private collection)

the standardization of panels on this led to some odd arrangements where outer walls had doors that led nowhere. Originally of stained timber, the further overpainting of some led to a scruffy appearance that overrode any architectural qualities they may have had. Only a few of these remain such as the signal box at Evesham.

Modernization

The 1950s saw the BTC take steps to modernize the railway system as well as repair it as there was an acknowledgement that passengers and commercial users were beginning to look to other modes for their transportation needs. Knowing that design was to play a key part in attracting custom, BTC set up a design panel under the chairmanship of Christian Barman. Whilst this paid some respect to architecture it was generally preoccupied with passenger train services and the shipping facilities within the commission.

In response to the need for electrification and route enhancement, the rebuilding programme led to architectural opportunity and the 1950s and early 1960s saw the design of many new station buildings such as Stafford, Banbury and Euston. Some of these are now regarded as architecturally significant and indeed have been listed as such. These include Harlow and Broxbourne stations (completed in 1960), Barking Station (completed in 1961), Birmingham New Street signal box and telephone exchange (completed in 1965), Manchester Oxford Road Station (completed in 1960) and Coventry Station completed in 1962. There were, of course, many other buildings instigated by regional and central offices and, of the earlier nationalized period buildings, some, such as the Rail Technical Centre administrative buildings (completed in 1965), Plymouth Station and signal box (completed in 1961) and modest offices buildings for divisional staff such as those at Shrewsbury (completed in 1961) clearly define railway architecture of the period.

As part of the Kent coast electrification and remodeling between Brighton and Portsmouth, the Southern Region designed two notable small stations at Folkestone and Chichester during the 1950s. However, the region will probably always be remembered for

Coventry, like Harlow of two years earlier, embraced an oversailing roof that visually connected all elements of the station, segregated passengers from goods and oriented those departing the station towards the city centre and its symbolic cathedral. Completed in 1962, it is now Grade II listed. (Photo: Paul Childs)

its later adoption of a proprietary modular building system usually used for housing, schools' offices and factories, known as 'CLASP' (Consortium of Local Authorities Special Programme) which was utilized for a number of stations in its rebuilding programme of the later 1960s.

Other smaller stations of note and rebuilt during this period were Macclesfield, East Didsbury, Potters Bar and Hadley Wood. Whilst seemingly undistinguished, Macclesfield does contain an unnoticed but rather elegant concrete footbridge structure typical of the period, although the station has again now been compromised by unsympathetic but inevitable later accretions. Potters Bar main station building was replaced by an office development but did include well-designed concrete canopies and, debatably, one of the best-looking signal boxes of the early 1950s.

Stations were not the only operational buildings of note during this period. Signal boxes and various control rooms were also architecturally significant and whilst Birmingham New Street is highly acclaimed, those of the Eastern Region at Potters Bar, Harlow, Ware and Broxbourne have a striking simplified form entirely related to their function, dominated by their oversailing roof line, which protects the windows from direct sunlight and mirrors the forms constructed at Harlow Station a few years earlier.

Unfortunately, many well-designed but under-appreciated control offices and towers associated with the hump and marshalling yards at places like Margam, Tinsley, Temple Mills and Healey Mills have been demolished. These had many similar attributes to airport control towers with designs entirely driven by functionality. Whilst striking in appearance, they were generally of load-bearing brickwork although Tinsley is of a prefabricated panel structure. All had oversailing flat roofs shielding glazed control rooms, which required full visibility of the yard below.

Reshaping – the Beeching Report

Following what were deemed to be failures to economize during the modernization programme, it was inevitable that the industry as a whole was reviewed, particularly in the face of increased competition from commercial and private road transport. This task fell to Dr Richard Beeching who had been appointed as chairman of the BTC in 1961. The government instructed him to prepare recommendations for the future of the railway system. The final report to this end entitled *The Reshaping of British Railways* was published in 1962 and the report, its implications and the subsequent implementation of the recommendations made have been the subject of heated discussion and debate ever since.

In essence, the report recommended closing unprofitable and little-used lines, particularly branch lines, to create a streamlined 'inter-city' network of passenger and freight routes. Thus, the largest and most significant and abrupt change to the extent of the railway estate and infrastructure came about in the years between 1963 and 1970 when the country saw the withdrawal of services from approximately 5,000 route miles of track and the closure of many supporting buildings, including nearly 50 per cent of the existing station stock remaining at the time of the report. There is still debate as to whether this action saved the railway system in the face of the unstoppable growth of road transport, which had seen a trebling of demand in the ten years prior to the report, or was, indeed, an act of short-term and unnecessary desecration never to be recovered from. It should not go unnoticed that the significant reduction in the workforce also had an impact on the need for building accommodation related to them and their work.

When viewed from a position in the twenty-first century where rail patronage has been growing, if unexpectedly, from privatization onwards, it is, perhaps, easy to be wise but personal and commercial travel planning from the early 1950s onwards was indicating a decline in rail patronage well in advance of Beeching's recommendations and, to many, the initiative, and the implementation of it, put it on a firm footing for survival.

The management of the railways was restructured after the report and the multi-transport interests of the BTC were dispersed. The railway infrastructure and operations now came under a new board – the British Railways Board, later to have a new corporate identity, and the British Railway Property Board, which became responsible for many rail-related commercial developments via developers and their appointed architects. The aim of the projects was to generate income whilst simultaneously facilitating upgraded stations. However, the integration of consultancy-driven commercial development with industry-driven station elements did not necessarily produce the most distinguished architecture of the period and certainly led to some of the stations losing an architectural identity or character of their own. Stations such as London's Cannon Street and Blackfriars, Bracknell, Watford and Swindon befell this fate, but similar compromise was to be seen in many cities across the UK. However, the 1960s Cannon Street Station development designed by John Poulson has since been replaced with a design by Foggo Associates and Blackfriars Station has been totally remodelled to span the Thames with its architectural character dominated by the roof over its platforms rather than its entrance buildings.

The role of chief architect that was set up at the outset of the BTC continued with the responsibility to the new British Railways Board although the regional architect's teams within the regions remained under the administration of the Regional Civil Engineers until the reorganization of the 1970s.

Whilst *The Reshaping of British Railways* did not refer directly to buildings, other than the schedules of stations to be taken out of service, not all of which comprised buildings, it is interesting to note that the newly formed British Railways Board was publicly promoting good design across its diverse services, particularly in respect of passenger trains. To this end, a number of exhibitions were held, the most prominent being the 'New Design for British Railways'

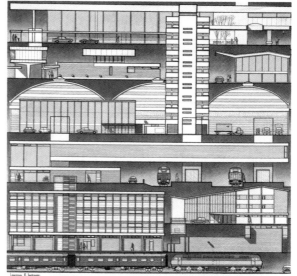

British Rail architect Lawrence Jackman's design for the poster that accompanied the exhibition held at the Building Centre in 1963 to celebrate the architecture of the period. This was a time of major reorganization and rebranding of the railway industry. Seen in the image are Manchester Piccadilly, Coventry, Banbury and Broxbourne stations together with Harlow Mill signal box. The exhibition was opened by the chairman of British Rail, Dr Richard Beeching. (Image: Private collection)

exhibition at the Building Centre in 1962 and the exhibition at the Design Centre in 1965 in connection with the launch of the newly formed BR's corporate identity programme, There was an optimism about these exhibitions that is not necessarily shared by those opposed to the background cuts in services and the uncertain futures of many fine buildings.

The impact of the Beeching report on the fortunes of railway buildings or indeed architectural design direction are a little hard to establish. The report was written at a time when the railway enterprise had to respond to commercial and general public demand for other forms of transport. It is possible that most of the work that the architects were dealing with during this period was on the lines being retained following the recommendations in the report and certainly the bigger projects, such as Birmingham New Street, Manchester Piccadilly and Euston, were well in hand at this time.

Now one of the liveliest meeting places in central Birmingham after recent redevelopment, Birmingham New Street was probably the least successful of all the 1960s joint development and station collaborations from an architectural point of view. The original work relegated the station, from being one of the grandest in the land, to a two-level interchange located beneath a shopping centre and multi-storey car park, neither of which were architecturally distinguished.

Euston Station Rebuilding Controversy

The most controversial construction project of the period, and the one that dominated the architectural headlines of the time was the rebuilding of Euston Station, coupled, as this was, with the required demolition of Hardwick's Great Hall and Doric Arch, which was located slightly north of the proposed terminating positions of the new track layout resulting from the new electrification works. It was inevitable that the debate surrounding this demolition would influence all subsequent architectural judgement of the station itself. However, one must remember that the station was a pioneering attempt at improving passenger comfort and convenience at a terminal station and was only the second major British city terminal of this scale to be built in the twentieth century. The concourse building has, even in recent years, been described as a concrete monstrosity and likened to the inside of a washing machine or, derisorily, an airport terminal. It has also been criticized for being designed by faceless bureaucrats but some would say that it is perhaps worthy of higher analysis than that.

Objectively, it can be described as none of these things. Yes, it might be akin to a modern airport in that it was intended to provide comfortable facilities with all information and useful amenities to hand in a light, bright environment but it was also designed to separate the handling of parcels, mail and train

The concourse at Euston, conceived with a lofty roof, perimeter glazing and views out towards the square to the south, which, within ten years of opening, were obscured by the construction of four independent but visually related commercial office blocks, one of which sits astride a major bus interchange. (Image: Private collection)

London's Euston Station shortly after opening in 1968 and aligned centrally with the LNWR war memorial as viewed from the Euston Road. The positioning of the later commercial development and the interrelated bus-station location effectively blocked this view as did the hotels and other buildings of the earlier-designed Philip Hardwick Station and entrance arch. (Photo: Private collection)

servicing arrangements from passenger movements, and was almost alone at the time for attempting this. It also had arrangements to allow baggage to be collected and transported so that passengers did not need to carry it around on their person.

It is a concrete building but one clad in marble, mosaic and hardwood although these are now either covered over or subject to temporary safety repairs. The let-down is the platform environment although this hardly gets a mention in any criticism of the station, which is almost entirely focused on the concourse building that stands as the visible sign of the replacement of the Arch. So, then, a bold concept for the concourse building but flawed as a whole and forever tainted by the destruction of the Arch and, perhaps, the later positioning of the Seifert and Partners commercial office development between the concourse building and the public square to the south.

The controversy and debate surrounding the fortune of the Arch overshadowed much of the output from the railway architects of the remaining 1960s and 1970s. The outfall from this episode also influenced future consideration of historic architecture of every genre. Consequently, the Arch has become more symbolic of the conservation movement than perhaps any other building and, as such, has steered architectural conservation policy at an international level. It could be said that the Arch has become more potent in its influence after its demolition and that our current policy and view of heritage would not be as focused now if the Arch had remained in situ without the fight to retain it.

Station Improvements and Beyond

Following the advent of BR, the regional architectural resources took on the responsibility for the design of many new projects through the remainder of the 1960s and 1970s. These mainly consisted of station improvements but also included many other building types, such as signal boxes and control towers, offices, depots and even related transport projects such as the hovercraft terminal at Dover for 'Sea Speed'.

East Grinstead was one of just over forty stations rebuilt utilizing the CLASP system. The lack of flexibility and the restrictions imposed by the system in long-term use rendered a replacement necessary and under the National Station Improvement Programme (NSIP) this was provided by a new station building designed by architects Howard, Fairbairn, MHK in 2012 with the official opening in 2013. (Photo: Private collection)

The projects planned during the early era were influenced by the corporate desire to portray the railway as a forward-looking industry whilst still coping with a vast estate that was seen by many as past its best, inappropriate for contemporary use and too expensive to maintain. It is against this backdrop that many of the architectural initiatives came about and where so much controversy was encountered, especially in the most public of railway buildings, stations.

The outputs of the modernization programme had largely been completed by the mid-1960s although Euston wasn't to be officially opened until 1968. However, the many smaller stations that remained in service during the implementation of the Beeching proposals now needed attention. In the Southern Region more than 200 stations were deemed to require urgent modernization and the Southern Regional Architect took the bold move to adopt the existing CLASP system for this purpose. This was seen as a logical and pragmatic approach to the problem of replacing what were deemed to be totally outmoded station facilities that would have cost too much to convert to modern facilities.

The programme of rebuilding in such a manner drew to a close with only 40 of the planned 200 buildings completed. Whilst most are still standing some have now been replaced with new buildings to meet current needs such as Wokingham and East Grinstead, the latter having adopted and refined the modular principles developed by Network Rail in 2007.

Following the lessons encountered with the use of system buildings on the Southern Region and with further proprietary systems on the Western Region, where, for instance Oxford Station was rebuilt with a timber-framed assembly, two new approaches were taken to station design: a forward-looking approach

One of the forerunners of the glazed box approach to small-station design, completed at Bishops Stortford in 1963. The enclosure could allow for a similar structure to be built at a number of stations with internal arrangements such as the entrances, exits and ticket offices positioned to suit the site orientation. (Photo: Private collection)

based on future flexibility and a rationalized, traditional approach. The first of these saw steel-framed, glazed envelopes with modular interiors similar to the Eastern Region's earlier example at Bishops Stortford but known as D70 (Design for the Seventies) in the Southern Region and System for Change (SFC) in the Eastern Region, with a typical example at Cheshunt. The second saw the development of traditionally built ticket offices around a common plan form as at New Beckenham and Teynham. The plan form of the latter went on to form the core of many regional variations where a rationalized, traditional approach was taken and pitched roofs were reintroduced to counter the failures many flat roofs experienced during this period.

The most prominent of the original D70 stations are at Maze Hill and Liss in Hampshire. Whilst Liss is still in its original form, albeit slightly cluttered by later equipment and other operational paraphernalia, Maze Hill has received partial over-cladding and cannot be seen as a clear concept now. Another example was completed at Elmers End where the principle was also integrated into the adjacent canopy construction. Adaptations of D70 can be seen at Streatham and the structural principles of this approach were later to

form what became known as OD70 (Office Design for the Seventies). Ten OD70 structures were planned and built at sites such as Basingstoke, Winchester, Fleet and Chichester. These are still standing but are almost unrecognizable now, having been partially clad, repainted or otherwise altered and adapted.

The glass-box approach allowed for flexibility

One of a small number of offices built for 'area' management during the 1970s and 1980s using the early D70 station-design principles. Whilst still standing, most of these, such as this one at Basingstoke, have been over-clad, altered or repainted so as to be unrecognizable from the original concept, which like the stations allowed for flexibility in planning the interior spaces. (Photo: Julian Wormleighton)

Winnersh Triangle was one of the first 'VSB90' station buildings. This new station site, just outside Reading, was also selected to house a DSB waiting shelter and seating at the platform level following an experimental collaboration with their chief architect, Jens Nielsen.

in planning the interiors and was also adopted by the London Midland Region at Radlett and the much bigger rebuilding of Bedford Station. Radlett incorporated a GRP ticket-sales unit from proprietary supplier Glasdon, thus adding to the modular nature of the design.

The 1960s and 1970s saw the railway architects tackle a diverse range of building projects, including the design of office tower blocks for a railway industry reorganization that didn't transpire. The tower near Birmingham New Street known as Stanier House and the office at York known as Hudson House (recently demolished) were part of this programme. Amongst the stations of the 1970s, Birmingham International is one of the biggest projects, linking the railway to Birmingham Airport and the newly completed National Exhibition Centre (NEC) via an over-track concourse. This aspect of the design dominates the planning and gives the building its distinctive character.

The 'Park and Ride' concept for a station took root in the 1970s at New Pudsey and the Western Region followed suit with a temporary trial at Bristol Parkway. This soon took hold with demand for a number of rebuilding programmes into the 1980s and 1990s. On the back of this success, the Western Region built a further facility at Tiverton Parkway in the 1980s.

The move for the very small stations to adopt a traditional design in the later 1980s moved forward with a semi-standardized approach known as VSB90 (very small buildings for the 1990s). This picked up the success of a number of individual buildings developed by the regional architect's office and formed the backbone of a number of successfully delivered projects, particularly in the south and Midlands at stations such as Winnersh Triangle near Reading and Tile Hill near Coventry.

The regional architect for the London Midland Region designed the new station at Milton Keynes, which opened in 1982. The main entrance formed part of a glass-clad office block fronting a square for transport interchange purposes. The entrance concourse is at bridge-deck level and stairs and lifts drop to the midpoint of platforms. The architecture of the station is seamless with the design ethos of the office block and, indeed, the central city architecture. Together with Birmingham International, these two stations were unusual at the time for being located entirely on new sites, most other station work of the period being the renewal of existing assets.

The crisp, clean lines of Milton Keynes Station and the use of mirror glass in the canopy fascias and light-coloured ceramic tiling reflects the design of the new office block over the main entrance: this in turn is seamless with the architecture of the city centre. (Photo: Paul Childs)

Woolwich Arsenal Station is one of the last stations to be designed by British Rail's Architecture and Design Group at the close of the nationalized period. The semi-circular forms at the extremities of the plan together with the glazed circular lantern share similarities with the Group's work at Ashford for the international services. (Photo: Paul Childs)

Perhaps the most significant project of the period for the BR in-house architectural teams was the reconfiguring of Liverpool Street Station, which is a tour de force of conservation work, railway remodelling, traditional new build and city planning. Few visitors would know that most of what they see before boarding trains dates from the end of the 1980s and is not Edward Wilson's nineteenth-century work. The introduction of a new transept to provide space for a new concourse makes the most significant contribution to the replanning of the station but what carries it off is the faithful replication of the constructional detailing found in the original structures, which remain towards the Exchange Square end of the station. These can be identified by the discoloured glazing and brown and cream paintwork.

This project set a new benchmark for station planning in the context of existing buildings and changed the direction of station-architecture conservation thereafter. BR's Architecture and Design Group who were responsible for both the station and the nearby signal control centre went on to design Woolwich Arsenal Station and Ashford International Station immediately afterwards.

Architectural Management

The 1980s saw a major change in the way that architecture and design was managed within BR. From having an organization that could design almost any project that the industry could request, the architectural resources were transformed under new directorship into two groups. One remained as a multi-disciplinary practice and the other, which was much smaller, formed itself into a group of design managers with the expectation that the design work would be contracted out and managed by them. This second group was honed to respond to the needs of the newly formed business sectors such as Network Southeast, InterCity, Regional Railways and Railfreight.

The practice group continued to work for railway clients on the aforementioned projects and the latter group concentrated on setting design standards and guidance to be adopted by appointed consultants and contractors. A particular success of this approach was the launch of the Network Southeast business and its brand. The design managers worked with the brand consultants to provide a guide to the selection of building materials, signage, colours, station equipment and furniture, and a pioneer project was rolled out at Richmond Station with many others set

Troughton McAslan's design for Redhill Station, completed in 1990 for Network SouthEast, was a bold change from the rationalized traditional designs concurrently being adopted for small stations. Whilst built as a steel-framed, glazed structure, it was inspired by the designs of Charles Hoiden's stations for London Transport sixty years earlier. (Photo: Peter Cook)

to follow suit at all stations within the business. The architectural response quickly transformed the image of the business and the stations within its portfolio following its brand launch in 1986. The immediate success of this inspired the other businesses to follow suit.

The sector architects were responsible for the design management of a number of stations, two examples being Tottenham Hale Station by Alsop and Lyall, and Redhill by Troughton McAslan – one of the first projects on the railway network for this practice. In 1997 John McAslan and Partners, and Ove Arup and Partners were to be appointed for the redevelopment of King's Cross station, a project that finally saw completion in 2012 but went through many development variations. Similar approaches by the other newly formed railway businesses followed suit with the sector architects each producing design guidance appropriate to the businesses they were aligned to. Special projects architects were also designated to manage the design development of major proposals at King's Cross and Waterloo, which were both related to the introduction of international train services to the UK.

In respect of these two proposals, Foster Associates (later Foster and Partners) were commissioned by the London Regeneration Consortium as 'masterplanners' for the railway lands but also independently by BR for the station-specific element of the overall project.

In the event, the project would be overtaken by the proposal to utilize St Pancras Station as the second international terminal and the original proposals were abandoned. Sir Norman Foster was later appointed as masterplanner with Rail Link Engineering for the remodelling of the station to accommodate the revised train services, his only other mainline railway work during this period being the station at Stansted Airport.

Waterloo International, now reopened after a period of closure as an extension to the 'domestic' services, was the last of the significant projects prior to privatization and was designed by Nicholas Grimshaw and Partners in conjunction with Sir Alexander Gibb and Partners, and YRM Tony Hunt Associates Ltd.

A pioneering design that had much in common with an iceberg, the majority of the complex planning and design was undertaken below platform level and within the arches beneath the existing station. This was the first time that complex customs and security arrangements had been integrated into a railway station in the United Kingdom. The curved and narrowing nature of the site on the northern edge of the existing station led to a sinuous form for the roof over the platform area. The ambition to create a single-span roof for the full length of this site led to a unique glazed solution that allowed regularly shaped panes to overlap and move semi-independently to take up any movement of the structure.

The construction of a single-span roof over the former international station platforms at Waterloo met the challenge of covering a long, sinuous and tapering site in a way that reflected the ingenuity and pioneering design of the large train sheds of the mid-nineteenth century. It was completed in 1994. (Photo: Robert Thornton)

Chapter Seven

The Privatized Period – 1994–2019

A Change of Direction

The move from a nationalized industry to a privatized one was complex. It commenced in 1994 although some transfer arrangements were phased over a three-year period up to 1997. Following privatization, the core operational railway transferred to one infrastructure company and a number of train operators, freight operators and rolling-stock leasing companies, each with varying degrees of architectural interest in the buildings for which they were now responsible.

Railtrack became the first to take up the role of infrastructure manager until 2001 when, following a period of administration, Network Rail was appointed to take it to the present day.

As the incoming 'landlord' of the infrastructure, Railtrack had the biggest long-term interest in property management, maintenance and development.

The operators and occupiers had the responsibility for day-to-day management and care of their own businesses, which included some maintenance responsibilities but also allowed them to present or modify their buildings as they wished. This meant that they could 'brand' them, fit them out and sign them to their own corporate standards.

The only constant visual reminder that one was embarking on a nationally connected system of transport from this point onwards was the obligatory use of the former British Rail logotype, now to be known as the National Rail symbol, at the approach or entrance to each passenger station.

Following privatization, tranches of investment have been led by the governments of the day to enhance passenger accessibility and facilities, and to encourage the use of trains as a mode of transport, given national sustainability and energy usage aspirations.

Like most of the major station roofs nationally, the entire roof at Edinburgh Waverley has been restored throughout, including the restoration of the circular, wrought-iron framed lantern over the central waiting area. A protective grid has been constructed above but this cannot be seen from the concourse. (Photo: Robert Thornton)

The consequence is that the portfolio overall looks very different to the one that was inherited by the private rail companies in 1994, despite the previous good work of the BR business sectors. The fragmentation of the industry has also led to inconsistencies of architectural approach and outlook that previous administrations had tried hard to avoid.

The number and diversity of architectural projects that have been completed in the period since privatization commenced is extensive and justice cannot be done to the scale of this work in these pages. Nearly every station and operational building has been impacted and stations, in particular, have been the beneficiaries of improvements related to better customer facilities, repairs, renewals and capacity enhancement. These benefits have taken place across the spectrum of buildings from the smallest, such as Grange over Sands and Mortimer, to the larger flagships such as Glasgow Central, Edinburgh Waverley, King's Cross and St Pancras, which have all seen transformation in the context of significant heritage buildings. Encouragingly, there have also been new station openings on existing and reinstated routes such as Oxford Parkway near Bicester and Buckshaw Parkway near Chorley.

Major infrastructure alterations have offered both challenges and opportunities as exemplified by the most recent of large-scale developments at London Bridge and Reading. Here, significant changes in track layout and train services led to the rebuilding of stations with the opportunity to improve connections between communities physically divided by rail infrastructure. It is difficult to compare the outlook of the railways in 1994 with the outlook today but the consequences of the investment in stations in particular has been a largely unrecognized and unheralded story for all those interested in railway architecture.

One of the unexpected demands on the railway system during this period has been the growth in passenger business, with demand nearly doubling over twenty-five years. The groundwork for this may have been during the sectorization of the nationalized period but the consequences for the infrastructure have been felt in this later period. The design of stations has had to keep up with demands for space, accessibility and functionality, any failings of which can affect the performance and capacity of the operational network.

Unlike previous periods, tracking the involvement and engagement of architects in building projects in this era is difficult, especially as they are widely dispersed. Certainly, the trend that started in the nationalized period to engage architectural consultants rather than utilizing in-house resources continued with most architectural consultancies reporting through contractors or project managers, the favoured route for most projects being via the contractors appointed for each stage of a job.

Early Privatization 1994–2001

When Railtrack took over the management of the railway infrastructure in 1994 it established a property directorate that took on all of BR's property interests under one umbrella. Previously, commercial property and operational property interests had been under separate command. Now there was an opportunity to unite all property-related skills, including architectural design management, into one organization. The closure of the nationalized period saw the end of BR's Directorate of Architecture Design and Environment with the element known as the Architecture and Design Group at first practicing on its own account and then under the name of Nick Derbyshire and Associates, which was absorbed into a larger engineering consultancy, Sir Alexander Gibb and Partners. The smaller group of business-related architects either went into the newly privatized rail companies or Railtrack where they were later united as a single team in the property directorate. They worked closely with the project delivery teams and the appointed architectural consultants and contractors to achieve company design ambitions through waves of buildings programmes including the architecturally significant Station Regeneration Programme (SRP).

Glasgow Central was a major beneficiary of SRP funding. The roof elements were completely restored by local architects Gordon Murray and Alan Dunlop. The teak 'torpedo' building to the side of the concourse, dates from 1879. However, the building to the left, which reproduces the form of this building, dates from the 1980s. (Photo: Paul Childs)

This period also saw a focus on station-specific investment between 1996 and 2001 that might have been diverted to other projects in the nationalized era. At the height of the SRP, which had an overall budget of £1.2 billion, many architectural practices were engaged throughout the country. Whilst not widely recognized, the industry had, as a result of this and other initiatives, become one of the biggest clients of architectural resources at this time.

Whilst later completed major projects in London have taken the limelight, it should be noted that major restoration works at places as diverse as Glasgow Central, Edinburgh Waverley, Brighton, Manchester Piccadilly, Newcastle Central, Cardiff Central and Bournemouth all benefited significantly during this programme as well as much smaller stations such as Hertford East, Harlow, Aberystwyth, Grange over Sands, Great Malvern, Wemyss Bay, Wellingborough and Blackburn. In all, more than 2,000 stations and more than 70 depots received attention.

From the outset, Railtrack managed both property and operations at the designated 'major stations',

Manchester Piccadilly was transformed in time for the 2002 Commonwealth Games. Its position in the city and the transport connections it provides were vital to the success of the Games. Unlike its cramped and inward-looking predecessor, the exterior of the station is outward-looking and visibly connects with its environment in daytime or at night. (Photo: David Barbour/Building Design Partnership)

Paddington concourse and Lawn were transformed in the late 1990s to provide a Heathrow Airport baggage check-in and enclosed waiting area for passengers. The works included the reinstatement and restoration of decorative ironwork in the Brunel shed gables. Architects Nicholas Grimshaw and Partners aligned the Lawn structures with the central shed span and created uninterrupted views along its length. (Photo: Robert Thornton)

later to be called 'managed stations', and when a separate division was created for this purpose, the London-based architects formed a small group in this team where they were to establish design guidance and work closely with appointed architects and designers on all projects including SRP, longer-term planning proposals and branding and signage initiatives. It was at this time that larger-scale projects, such as the remodelling of King's Cross Station, were launched and the architects were appointed, although it was another thirteen years and many changes of direction before the final scheme there was opened to the public.

With focused teams of station managers, project delivery teams and in-house architectural advisors, much significant work was undertaken, often marrying diverse projects on single sites to great advantage. Manchester Piccadilly is one such example. Here, restoration of historic elements of the station by architects EGS Design under SRP were coupled with the rebuilding of the concourse and the integration of the Manchester tram links, all completed in time for the Commonwealth Games in 2002 and undertaken without disruption to existing services. Leeds is another good example where a resignalling programme was coupled with the opportunity to remove the old 'agricultural' portal-framed shed, restore and reuse

the 1930s Art Deco former concourse and reorganize traffic and pedestrian access to enhance capacity and provide better customer facilities. The Building Design Partnership (BDP) team commisioned for the Manchester Piccadilly concourse rebuilding went on to redesign the concourse and restore the adjacent buildings at Manchester Victoria in 2014.

This programme made a huge difference to the vitality and appearance of stations of all scales and this impact was further augmented by funding from the Railway Heritage Trust for detail work on listed structures. It also saw a general change in the way that architects were engaged on railway projects with them now becoming part of contractor's teams, supplying a turn-key product. In some instances, notably at Paddington, where Grimshaw had been appointed directly by Railtrack for the early stages of a station-design programme, the practice was novated to the contractor and a client contact remained in place throughout Phase One of the works at the station. These works embraced the Lawn redevelopment as the baggage-handling facility for the newly introduced Heathrow Express services and the restoration of key heritage features in the station such as the decorative wrought-iron scrollwork in the shed gables. This reconfiguration and restoration formed the initial part of a carefully staged redevelopment of the station, which focused on the conservation and appreciation of Brunel's original work.

Later Privatization 2003–19

The major structural changes to the management of the railway infrastructure precipitated by the demise of Railtrack, the appointment of an administrator and consequential birth of Network Rail only marginally changed the way that architects within and without the infrastructure company worked. It should also be noted that certain train operating companies and passenger transport executives also engaged architects and engineers to design buildings and elements, such as ticket offices, within their own portfolios. The stations on the Mersey Rail system, such as St Helens and Sandhills, are good examples of this.

Except for property development projects, most consultant architects were now being engaged directly by project management teams or contractors with the in-house architects and property managers providing design briefs and design review services for live projects. Behind the scenes, the company architects were still busy reviewing and creating appropriate design standards on a range of building matters, particularly those relating to the larger stations, such as safety, accessibility, capacity, sustainability and heritage.

The need for an architectural resource in Network Rail found itself first in the property directorate and then in the asset management function where the role of Head of Station Design was created. The title quickly changed to Principal Architect so that the outputs of the team could apply to all buildings and not just stations. The changeover from Railtrack to Network Rail also saw the creation of an architectural design capability in the project delivery division. This team was responsible for a number of projects at both design and implementation stages including stations at Rochester and it was also responsible for the later initial design development of the new operational control centres, the first of which was completed on site at Three Bridges near Crawley in 2014.

Larger Projects

Many of the larger projects in the infrastructure portfolio had their origins in earlier phases of railway planning or development, namely, those connected with Crossrail and Thameslink. Whilst those relating to the larger Crossrail stations are yet to be seen, a smaller one at Abbey Wood is now open to the public.

The three significant Thameslink stations with their origins in the nationalized period, but which were constructed during this period are those at Blackfriars, London Bridge and Farringdon, although

London Blackfriars provides access on both riverbanks: the first station to do so. It also provides the finest views of London from its platforms. A project with a long design history encompassing stages by Allsops and Jacobs, and executive support as at other stations from Pascall and Watson. (Photo: Robert Thornton)

The juxtaposition of old and new at St Pancras provides new entrances to Midland Road, Pancras Road and an interchange to Thameslink and the Underground services below. The station track layout was widened and lengthened beyond the capabilities of the existing station, the design of the whole being a collaboration of the design consortium Rail Link Engineering and master planner Foster and Partners. (Photo: Robert Thornton)

the dedicated station beneath St Pancras shouldn't go unmentioned. All of different scale and with their own operational parameters, they are key in the development of railway architecture and all have regenerative and civic implications above their immediate functionality. This is particularly true of Blackfriars and London Bridge. Blackfriars unites two sides of the River Thames and in no small way contributes to the success of the South Bank as a cultural destination, while London Bridge unites two sides of a London borough that was bisected by a virtually impenetrable railway viaduct.

With the growing need for European interoperability of train services, attention was also diverted to the collaboration needed for internationally agreed design standards for disabled travellers, culminating in the issue of the TSI-PRM (Technical Specification for Inter-operability for Persons with Reduced Mobility), one of the cornerstones of station design.

The conversion of St Pancras Station into the second channel tunnel-connected terminal was completed in 2007 and the new facilities were officially opened on the 6th November of that year by HM Queen Elizabeth II. It is difficult to imagine that this building was close to being demolished in the 1960s and was languishing as a station until the start of this project. The completion of the second phase of Channel Tunnel rail links into the capital, which saw fast domestic services running on the same lines into the station, has given new life, purpose and impetus to the building, transforming every aspect of its operations including a new interchange with the Thameslink services and the London Underground beneath the station. It represents a major step forward in the appreciation of railway heritage and, like Liverpool Street before it, has set a benchmark for conservation and regeneration in an essentially operational environment. It is no coincidence that Alastair Lansley was the key architect for both of these projects.

Together with the completion of King's Cross Station and the major connections these two have, with the unsung and unseen reconfigured underground network, enabled the transformation of the adjacent railway lands to the north.

The West Midlands has also seen the transformation of Birmingham New Street Station in a scheme designed by Atkins and the Foreign Office. The need to enhance station capacity at this major interchange station and the desire of the City authorities to find a new image for their gateway building whilst connecting physically separated quarters of the City led to the redevelopment of the entire station site. The key design aspiration to draw more light into the concourse level was achieved by removing the central section of the shopping-level floor. Unfortunately, this concept could not be taken down to platform level due to the need to keep separation from the type of trains on the services from the station.

Other Projects

Mention should also be made of other station projects on the mainline rail network. In this period there have been many partnership projects with local planning authorities and passenger transport executives. In the north-west, a number of stations have been rebuilt or substantially modified on Mersey Rail, Sandhills and St Helens being two examples. The earlier station at St Helens designed by the BR London Midland Region in 1961 was a showcase for local glass company Pilkingtons, and the replacement completed in 2007 is an equally interesting showcase in a plan form that focuses on the main axis into the town. The architects SBS also completed the station at Accrington, which embraced many sustainability credentials and was one of the first stations to be awarded a BREEAM (Building Research Establishment Environmental Assessment Method) 'Excellent' rating.

Chiltern Railways has been a pioneer in developing an independent approach to its services and its stations. The restoration of Moor Street is exemplary, but it has also built new stations at Warwick Parkway, Haddenham and more recently Bicester Village where its links to the station at Oxford are further extending its range and popularity.

The opening up of Liverpool Lime Street Station frontage is a major demonstration of how important a station building can be to the quality of the urban environment. The removal of the tower block and the single-storey row of shops masking the station gable, together with the imaginative landscaping of the public space in front of the station has transformed the quality of the adjacent public domain.

It is worth mentioning three other initiatives that have taken place during this period, generated by the Department for Transport and coordinated through the Rail Delivery Group. These have all contributed significantly to the development of station premises although entirely sympathetic architectural solutions have sometimes proved elusive given the constraints imposed by some of the operational sites.

The Access for All (AfA) Project, which was initiated in 2006, set out to deliver the mobility improvements at stations in compliance with the TSI-PRM initiative, now enshrined in European Standards. The prioritized work-stream first sought to introduce step-free access at those stations where no facility existed and to improve those significant stations where provision was deemed inadequate. Options included platform alterations to reduce 'stepping' distances, the introduction of additional and supplementary handrails to stairs and the introduction of ramps and lifts to improve access to bridges and subways. The

Forming part of the EU Sustainable Station Project, Accrington Station was opened in 2010 following a partnership of Lancashire County Council, Northern Rail, East Lancs Community Rail Partnership, Network Rail and Hyndburn Borough Council. (Photo: Gary Seed)

Liverpool Lime Street sits in a commanding position above the city and adjacent to St George's Hall. Following the 1960s development, the frontage was all but hidden from public view. (Photo: Robert Thornton)

listed station at Huddersfield was furnished with glazed lifts to the subway, whilst many other stations such as Twyford, Gravesend, Hereford and many more were treated to lifts in a variety of architectural styles. One of the most successful lift design solutions was that at Gleneagles Station where the existing architectural style was replicated in an extension of the existing building envelope.

A further continuing project, the NSIP (National Station Improvement Programme) was introduced to undertake improvements in station facilities and to improve the ambience of the station for customers. Waiting and toilet facilities were both addressed and the programme focused on the requirements of the train-operating companies, which were encouraged in association with Network Rail to produce proposals, which can be seen to provide improvements in an economic and measurable manner.

The removal of the frontage development and the rebuilding of a public space beneath the shed gable at Liverpool Lime Street has transformed the setting of the station and allowed it to regain its dominant position. The single-glazed gable above a stone arcade forms a dramatic backdrop for the terraces below. (Photo: Robert Thornton)

Gleneagles Station. Recently refurbished with the stair towers seamlessly extended in original form, in time for the Ryder Cup, to provide space for lifts to serve the footbridge. (Photo: Paul Childs)

Modularization

In an endeavour to build and maintain railway infrastructure more quickly and economically modularization has found particular favour for track and signalling applications. The adoption of modularized building methodology has yet to gain a widespread footing possibly because there is not the same demand for a 'repeat' structure as there is for the other mentioned products. However, Network Rail developed design concepts for a modular station in 2005 and a number of pioneering structures have been built, notably at Greenhithe and Corby.

The original concepts were developed into a design and specification standard by engineering group Jacobs for reference purposes but subsequent designs have sought to further develop localized nuances to suit clients, local communities and civic authorities. A number of successful derivatives have thus been completed and, whilst it is perhaps not immediately obvious, the principles of modular planning were used at West Hampstead in an imaginative interpretation by Landholt and Brown for Thameslink, and at Burgess Hill by Paul Beaty-Pownall (PBR Architects) for Southern Rail. The new station facilities at Deptford used the same principles to create a multi-level access to the platforms and the CLASP station at East Grinstead was replaced with a new station by Howard

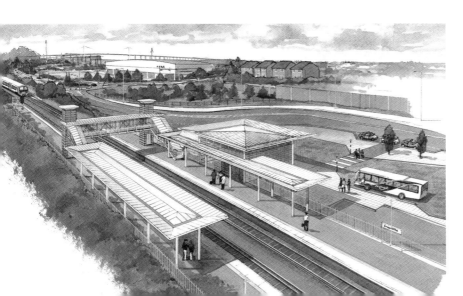

Part perspective of Network Rail's medium-scale modular station concept as envisaged for Greenhithe. It was intended that the materials used for the rainscreen form of cladding could be selected to suit the local environment. All elements were to be detailed with common components. (Drawing: Network Rail. Artwork commissioned from Henry Lambon)

Fairburn MHK following these same principles

The privatized era has seen the development of 'masterplans' for many station sites, particularly where commercial property opportunities arise, but the larger such projects are subject to market fluctuations and particularly those emanating from the global downturn of the early years of the millennium. However, where there have been overriding operational imperatives such as those related to the aforementioned Thameslink or Crossrail projects, great progress has been made although the architecture related to the central London Crossrail stations has yet to be unveiled.

In Scotland, the Edinburgh to Glasgow Improvement Programme (EGIP) has created the opportunity for major rebuilding at Glasgow Queen Street, due to be opened during 2020.

The era has also seen property wing of the infrastructure operator forming an innovative partnership with a property developer for the joint development of station-focused projects at outer London stations such as Epsom, Walthamstow and Twickenham.

Whilst not of the same overall scale as the combined projects at St Pancras and King's Cross, the works to transform operations at London Bridge are now unveiled and, despite their understated architecture, combine all elements of current architectural direction in the transport field with a skilful blending of historic sensitivity, innovative engineering, urban integration and operational understanding. The phased works were undertaken whilst the station remained fully operative, which is no small feat in a busy central London location.

The new concourse at London Bridge unites all platform areas at the station for the first time in its history and simultaneously connects the streets and communities on either side previously severed by the railway viaduct. (Photo: Paul Childs)

...hire & Yorkshire Railway stained glass - Manchester Victoria Station - RT 6 Nov

Chapter Eight

Types of Building

A Diverse Portfolio

With the growth of other forms of transport and communications, the prolonged life of the railway system in the UK has seen many of the activities requiring specialized buildings wax and wane with contemporary trends. From a period at the end of the nineteenth and beginning of the twentieth centuries, where railway companies managed every aspect of their business with their own resources and facilities to the current era where much of the production and services required to run trains are outsourced, the demand for buildings to support railway company operations has changed dramatically, as has the need for architects and engineers to design and build them.

Changes in the distribution of goods rendered many depots, goods yards and warehouses redundant and, of course, the reduction in track mileage had a corresponding impact on lineside building requirements such as for signal boxes and maintenance staff accommodation.

This section highlights the key building types that have made up the railway buildings portfolio over the years and, whilst acknowledging that those such as hotels are no longer generally part of railway company assets, it should be recognized that they would not have been created if it had not been for the railways and are therefore included here. Also referenced are a number of structures that are no longer needed for operational purposes, such as water tanks and towers, but which add significant architectural character to railway sites and are enjoying new life with new uses.

Stations

The word station has, in the past, been used to describe more than just the passenger buildings with which the word is now almost wholly associated. Whilst it might not always be recognized by today's passengers, station buildings, the uses to which they were put, and the sites they occupy, have changed greatly over the period of their existence, particularly in the years following World War II, when the distribution of many goods gradually transferred to an improving road network and the railways developed 'train-load' instead of 'wagon-load' distribution.

Station locations generally developed to embrace passengers as well as the railway company's goods and parcels business. The selected sites often incorporated extensive yards containing storage and trans-shipment buildings, various administrative offices and, in certain locations, specialized storage or provision for handling livestock and fresh produce. Depending on the location of the station there may also have been a requirement for locomotive and rolling-stock storage, turning, maintenance and refuelling. Many stations also had provision for coal merchants.

From the earliest days of the railway there was a need to provide domestic accommodation for the station master and other staff, and many of the small or medium-sized stations incorporated a station house. As passenger traffic grew and the distribution of goods transferred away from local stations the primary station buildings generally became focused on passengers and the goods traffic that more comfortably mixed with passenger traffic, such as parcels and mail, which continued into the 1990s. The later

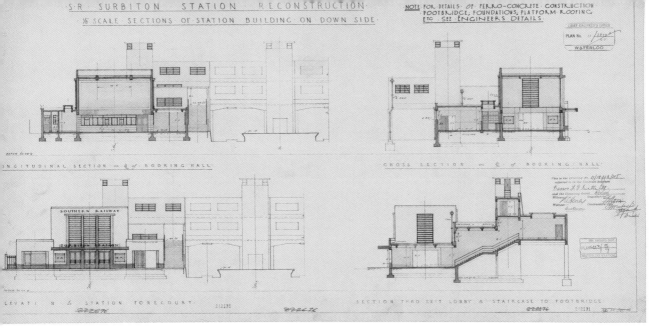

The working drawings for Surbiton show the separation of parcels and people, but it is the lift towers for parcel handling purposes that give this station much of its character, providing the opportunity to include prominent clock faces. (Drawing: Network Rail archive)

planning of stations took account of the separation of this traffic from passengers. An example can be seen in the 1930s design of Surbiton Station by the SR where a completely segregated system of link bridges, corridors and lift shafts were designed in. These features were even articulated or exaggerated in the development of later station designs such as for Stafford, Harlow and Broxbourne.

In the early years, all of this was of little concern, and most stations had little more than a water tower and coaling point, possibly a waiting room and staff accommodation. They were often single-sided facilities and even when second platforms were added, footbridges and subways were a thing of the future, with most access across the tracks being by level-barrow crossings.

Stations are now predominantly focused on passengers, all other types of traffic having ceased to operate or having moved to specialist depots elsewhere on the network. In recent years, stations have been categorized by the range and type of facilities present, particular those related to accessibility and safety. This progression to passenger-focused stations has led to some redundancy in station buildings

and finding productive use has, in many cases, become challenging.

The advent of ticketing, and particularly the widespread introduction from 1842 of the Edmondson card-ticket system, originally used on the NCR, was the moment when ticket offices became more sophisticated in terms of planning, and distinct classes of travel became more standardized. This in turn led to the duplication of facilities such as waiting rooms, in one building, albeit designed and fitted out to different standards. This led to a change in scale in the architecture of the medium-sized stations, which now needed to cover goods and mail handling, and in many rural areas the transportation of livestock or specialized goods. The result was an expansion of the land needed for station operations, thus eventually having a significant implication for the status of the station and the consequential impact on the local environment.

The need for passengers to buy a ticket to travel has been at the core of passenger-station design for as long as trains have been running. However, in more recent years the ability for passengers to buy tickets from free-standing automated machines or, even

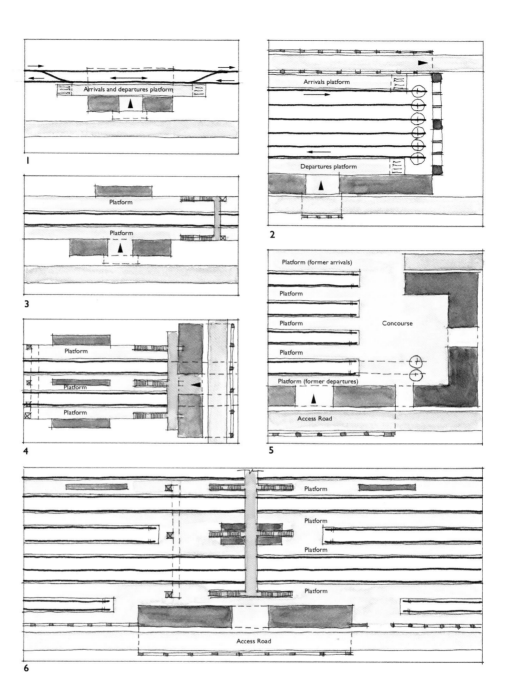

Diagrammatic representation of the three station types loosely based on known examples. 'Through' terminal and a combination of the two, can have implications for architecture, especially where footbridges are required. Here, 1–3 show through station arrangements; 4–5 show terminal arrangements; 6 shows a mixed 'through' and terminating arrangement. (Drawing: Robert Thornton)

more recently, online, has fundamentally changed the need for, and usage of, ticket offices as they are traditionally recognized. However, where these are deemed to be required, even if only for use at peak times, they are still planned around a secure counter position with cash transfer mechanisms, cash tills,

ticket issuing machines and so on. Computerization may have taken over many of these functions, but the resulting layout and planning of the ticket office has not significantly changed since a standard approach was adopted in the 1960s and 1970s when BR developed a modular layout embracing operational

The ticket office at Reading was one of the last designed in the nationalized period around the established ticket-issuing arrangements and before ticket-issuing machines became so familiar to users. Product design consultant Fitch & Co. with Paul Stead designed the prototype for implementation at Reading, which was officially opened by Her Majesty the Queen in 1989. (Photo: Paul Childs)

furniture specifically designed for the purpose.

The operational changes over the years have seen the original simplistic layout of many stations become more complex and the alterations have produced a variety of scales and arrangements. However, historically, stations generally conform to three basic arrangements outlined here, each of which has different operational characteristics and implications for passenger circulation and dwell times.

'Through' Stations

The 'through' station designation applies to the majority of stations encountered on the network. The earliest forms of station were in the main single-sided, although variations of layout occurred. The Liverpool and Manchester Railway adopted a workable arrangement of small buildings to provide basic facilities, with only Edge Hill with its winding engines and Manchester Liverpool Road terminus

being distinctly different. The GWR favoured a combination of buildings; one being a larger accommodation building and the other – usually opposite – a smaller shelter-based building. Brunel did, however, use an intricate layout for some of the larger stations, such as Slough, Reading and Taunton, where the building range was set on one side of the track with two pavilion structures on the same platform providing separate 'up' and 'down' station facilities. Trains crossed from one track to stand at the London-bound facility at one end of the platform, or if travelling away from London at the other end.

This methodology required trains to cross tracks and as operations increased this practice became unworkable with the result that a more traditional layout with an opposing set of platforms was developed. The progression to this layout included overall train-shed roofs with the platforms accessed by level-barrow crossings until footbridges and subways were included to improve safety.

The larger stations with additional platforms were

The through platforms at Reading have canopies that rise over the access deck located above them. This reinforces the important element of circulation and passenger distribution, thus giving the station its distinctive character. The canopies at London Bridge, by the same architect, provide a similar emphasis to the position of the concourse below. (Photo: Jon Cunningham)

not just the preserve of the GWR: the MR also produced stations with multiple islands such as those at Kettering, which were linked by a rudimentary subway. The later development of station layouts based on American systems is illustrated by Nottingham and Leicester, both of which were developed by Charles Trubshaw in the formative years of the twentieth century. Similar but earlier and smaller examples of this type of layout can be seen at Crystal Palace, Denmark Hill and Preston.

The designs generated by Trubshaw included a large porte-cochère to provide sheltered access to the station facilities spanning the tracks and platforms at street level. A distribution bridge provided access to the lower-level platforms. Changes in the pattern of station usage have now allowed the porte-cochère to be used as pedestrian circulation space.

Of the larger through stations, Reading and London Bridge have both been remodelled with a form of architecture by Grimshaw that strongly expresses the nature of their operations with the sweeping platform canopies emphasizing the location of the access deck in the case of Reading or the concourse below in the instance of London Bridge.

Terminal Stations

Terminal stations range from basic facilities at the end of a branch line such as at Henley-on-Thames to grander multi-track facilities such as at the London cathedral stations, Glasgow Central, Liverpool Lime Street or Hull Paragon. In the early years, some stations would have been provided with train arrival and station egress from one flank of the building and station access and train departure from the other flank. There would have been multiple tracks for storage and marshalling purposes between with no real need for the two types of passenger to mix. The original Paddington Station and King's Cross Station layouts were based on such a premise.

One of the key aspects of terminal stations is the requirement for a connecting concourse to distribute passengers to respective platforms. Although they

Norwich Thorpe Station only has terminating platforms and, like many stations of this type, where access is level with the platforms, it doesn't require subways or footbridges. Similar in operational scale to Aberystwyth, the platform areas are mainly protected by extended canopies. (Photo: Robert Thornton)

all have very different operational characteristics, Glasgow Central, London Waterloo, Aberystwyth, Brighton, Eastbourne all share this particular aspect. Even the branch line stations could be more than a simple termination, and Wemyss Bay, regarded as one of the most iconic terminal stations, has a character all of its own, but is based on this layout with the addition of an access way to the adjacent ferry terminal.

The terminal station generally feels different to a through station, particularly in regard to its urban context. It is generally more accessible, in that level changes are not needed to access trains and it does not have the effect of bisecting communities geographically. The presence of a forecourt can often present a dignified setting and a focus for regeneration of a wide area. A station such as Thorpe in Norwich has these architectural qualities and can thus be seen as a fine entrance to the city.

Mixed 'Through' and Terminating Stations

At some stations, large and small, a combination of through and terminating platforms can be seen, a smaller example being at St Erth in Cornwall, where

the London to Penzance mainline is joined by the branch from St Ives, and a larger example being at Edinburgh Waverley and York where the terminating platforms divide the through mainlines.

Similar scenarios occur at many stations, but the common factor is that they will all require either footbridges or subways at some position in the premises even if they have level-access concourse for some of the platforms. Where the through platforms are remote, as at Manchester Piccadilly, additional passenger facilities may be required. The distance between the two facilities in this instance are alleviated by the use of travelators connecting the two concourse areas: the first time that these had been used on the mainline network. A junction station such as Lewes where two lines converge but do not terminate, for example, where a branch line joins a mainline, could be regarded as a through station.

Functional Changes

All stations and the land around them have continually adapted, and sometimes altered significantly, in response to changes in functional requirements, particularly towards the end of the nationalized period.

York station has five through lines and five bay platforms, two of which are reached via level access from the main station entrance. The centrally positioned footbridge is supplemented by subways and lifts that were originally used for goods transfers. (Photo: Robert Thornton)

The movement of passengers is now the principal activity at most stations but it should be remembered that they were often designed to support diverse operational functions, sometimes over a twenty-four-hour period.

Typical central city locations, such as Paddington, Liverpool Street or Birmingham New Street, also once provided the transfer and passage of mail emanating from both the road network and, in the case of the former, dedicated underground railway. The position of the sub-platform conveyors and tunnel systems affected the physical layouts of these stations until this activity ceased in the late 1990s.

Stations also combined light goods operations contiguously with passenger operations particularly in respect of parcels. The barrows and wagons designed for concourse use during the nationalized period had an entirely appropriate acronym

Until the later 1990s, passengers shared concourse and platform space with all manner of operational equipment. This view from the 1950s shows the barrows used for the movement of parcels and mail, which were later replaced by caged utility vehicles know as BRUTES. These could be linked together and pulled by electric tugs. (Photo: Network Rail archive)

BRUTE (British Railways Universal Trolley Equipment). Whilst much bulk parcels traffic eventually ceased, the Red Star Parcels service, which utilized the storage facility available on passenger trains flourished until the 1990s but the conflict on platforms was perhaps less noticeable.

Other traffic that required the access of large road vehicles into stations, such as overnight newspaper distribution, also ceased when in the instance of Paddington and the other London Stations, Fleet Street production moved to other centres in the 1990s. Whilst many of these activities were not seen or experienced by the travelling public, they nonetheless put a straitjacket on the opportunities for station redevelopment at the time.

The primary demand on the station network is now the growth in passenger usage. However, space is at a premium and this together with the need to provide 'accessible' access for users of all abilities and across all station facilities is a priority in station planning. Designing and managing premises to this end in the context of existing facilities within physical constraints calls on sophisticated passenger modelling and planning techniques such as those adopted by Network Rail. This is particularly important when developing and planning infrastructure designs for the future when it is necessary for investment purposes to look forward twenty-five or thirty years.

There is an important link between station design and train design and performance, which is exacerbated on intense services. Speed of boarding and alighting can be affected by such things as canopy provision on platforms, the positioning of which can affect the disposition of passengers and their movements in wet weather. Also important at a microlevel is the positioning of passenger information and station signage.

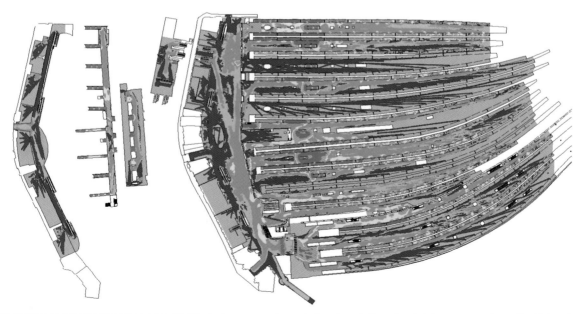

An example of the outputs of the Legion-Bentley systems computer analysis and modelling of pedestrian movements used by Network Rail during the design development of the ticket gates at Waterloo Station. The colour codes indicate relative densities of congestion or free flow, red indicating the most severe congestion at a particular time. (Image: Network Rail and Bentley Systems)

Signal Boxes

Functionality and Development

Signal boxes have been one of the most familiar, and indeed significant, railway buildings, embracing a unique architecture almost wholly driven by their function. Whilst signal-box designs have developed and been built through all the identified eras of railway history, they are mainly represented by what is regarded as the traditional box, for instance, those generally built prior to the railway Grouping. There are over 500 of this type still in existence, although it is recorded by English Heritage in a research report published in 2012 that there had been more than 10,000 prior to nationalization in 1948. Network Rail's plans to replace most of the remaining boxes with fourteen strategically placed operational centres is seeing a new breed of facility that triggers the further demise of the familiar boxes in a functional capacity.

They have derived as a form from the need to house manually operated levers connected to mechanical signals of various types and to the blades on track switches and turnouts. Generally positioned to the

The development of signal boxes has led to striking architectural forms, all of which (until the present day) have been derived from their functionality and proximity to the railway lines they control. The advent of advanced electronics and the ability to control large areas of the network from a single box have broken that specific relationship. See: 1: standard LNWR box; 2: standard LMS Scottish division cabin; 3: Canterbury West; 4: Woking; 5: Potters Bar; 6: Broxbourne; 7: London Bridge; 8: Colchester; 9: Network Rail design principles established for the latest Regional Operational Control Centres. (Drawing: Robert Thornton)

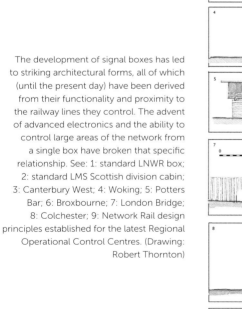
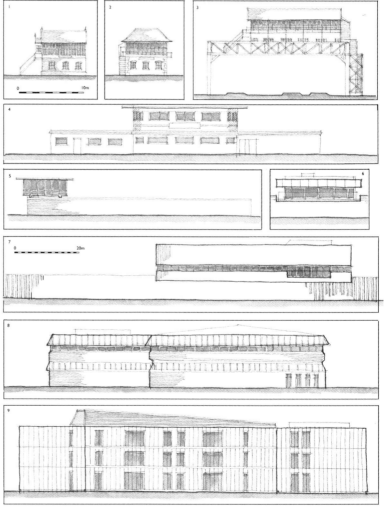

Originally built beside the track leading out of the station, the signal box at Liverpool Street, designed by BR's Architecture and Design Group, is now entirely surrounded by high-rise commercial buildings. In a complete design break with its forerunners, this centre is entirely clad in white-and-blue stove-enamelled panels. (Photo: Robert Thornton)

side of the track where the lever mechanisms could be conveniently connected to the point-operating rods, this proximity to operations has made reuse difficult in an era when these boxes are closing down and new uses are sought.

Whilst the lever frame still exists, the biggest change came about when the development of electromagnetic switching mechanisms was introduced, and all new boxes thereafter adopted this mode of operation. The traditional rationale for design then made way for a stripped-down functionalism that some observers may regard now as brutalist although perhaps only a handful of these latter ones could be described as such.

There are those that defy conventional architectural categorization such the signal box at Liverpool Street and Westbury Power Box. The later boxes have now combined with other operations to become much larger but even fewer in number and of less descriptive architecture externally.

Victorian and Edwardian Signal Boxes

The most commonly adopted structure for this purpose was designed and manufactured by John Saxby after he had established his system for 'absolute block' interlocking signalling and points systems. Whilst most of the railway companies adopted the basic principle, they also took advantage of the design options being offered by other suppliers.

Both levels were usually accessed by an external door and the lower level, which was often a brick structure, could be designed with several small windows to provide natural daylight. The locking equipment was carried on a separate structure of steel joists, which in turn carried the heavy lever-frame mechanism set at the upper- or operating-floor level. The operating floor would be glazed for at least 50 per cent of the elevations for full visibility of the track in 'up' and 'down' directions, with either brick- or timber-clad walls for the rest.

In most instances, toilet facilities, where they existed, would be located at ground-floor level. If

The Saxby & Farmer signal box in the Old Station at Bristol Temple Meads is a rare example of a bespoke design integrated within another building, this time being built partly in the train shed and partly outside. (Photo: Malcolm Wood)

most common sights was the introduction of various carpets and other forms of rudimentary insulation around the lever frame. The admirable initiative to redress these shortcomings was not put in place until the 1990s following privatization. Most boxes were provided with a cast-iron 'Tortoise' stove or in some later cases a small hearth. Access to the upper operating floor could be either by an external timber stair or by the luxury of an internal staircase where space constraints permitted.

Boxes could, of course, vary in size and complexity depending on the nature of the operations in the location they served. Some simple crossing boxes were particularly bijou, whilst those serving significant junctions or goods-yard systems could be of significant size. The former is exemplified by the small crossing box at Grain in Kent which serves a simple-goods branch, whilst at the other extreme, the iconic three-storey-high LNWR box at Shrewsbury Severn Bridge Junction, and the large box at Canterbury West, which spans the track on its own bridge structure, are fine examples.

The Signal Boxes of the Grouping Era

Signal boxes did not vary much in this basic form right through the Victorian era and into the Edwardian period, but after Grouping in 1923 some significant architectural changes occurred. One of the main changes came from the Southern Railway, where electrification of their network led to the need for new boxes for which a very futuristic approach to the architectural style of the structure was adopted. The signal boxes and electrification control centres were designed as solid brick structures, with curved corners and reinforced concrete canopies. Windows were mostly glazed with metal Crittall-style glazing systems, the glazing being generally in horizontal pane format, with curved corners expressed and an oversailing flat roof above the operating room. There was a desire amongst railway companies to represent speed and the aerodynamic form of these buildings

the signalman was really fortunate, he might have a facility at operating-floor level. Sometimes the toilet facility was in an adjacent building, particularly if the box was located near or within a station curtilage.

There was generally no separate ceiling, the sarking boards of the pitched roofs being the visible soffit of the roof space. With windows that generally required opening to enable the signalman to communicate with drivers, and with an open metal-lever frame at floor level, allied to permanently open ports in the walls at the foot of the box to enable cables and point rods to exit the box, it is no surprise that the boxes were not really energy efficient. One of the

The signal box at Woking typifies SR's approach to the signal boxes of the period, with the curved form of its control room and the box name in bold, sans-serif letters integrated into a horizontal concrete band that wraps around the upper tier of the structure and further enhances the horizontal emphasis. (Photo: Paul Childs)

expressed that mood most eloquently. This expression was aided by the fact that the lower of the two floors now needed to be bigger than the upper control level and the stepped arrangement started to take on the form of a streamlined ship rather than a traditional small building.

Not until the outset of World War II did signal boxes take on a more austere and functional style. This was partly due to the need to develop boxes capable of withstanding aerial bombardment. The LMS began to develop simpler brick signal boxes furnished with flat roofs, mainly in their North Western area, but developed a reinforced concrete-framed structure with screened entrances known as an ARP box, as exemplified (and still in place) at Runcorn in Cheshire. Glazing in order to maintain visibility of the railway continued to be extensive on the upper floor.

The Nationalized Period

The post-nationalization period saw little new development of boxes but continued with replacement of boxes lost in the war, based in the main on functional designs utilized previously although austerity measures, lasting well into the 1950s, had an influence on construction and materials selection.

By the mid- and late 1950s, as a result of the development of electronic signalling systems and the BR modernization programme, a bolder approach was taken. This system that followed on from the lead given by the SR saw the advent of a new form of signalling panel replacing the lever mechanisms of before with control being housed in a far more comfortable environment. As a result, larger areas of operation were controlled by one box, and the power signal box was born. These were generally much larger structures and were exemplified by remaining examples at Faversham, Cardiff, Saltley in Birmingham and Trent Valley near Nottingham.

The modernization programme, which embraced many track and operational upgrades, spawned a number of new boxes, all of which were designed by the emboldened architects' teams within the BR regional civil engineering offices. Of this period, some striking examples of a new approach could be seen at Potters Bar and Belford (completed in 1955) with designs by the Eastern Regional Architect and at Coventry by the Midland Regional Architect. The 'modern movement' styling of this period was also to be seen in the control towers' boxes in marshalling yards such as Temple Mills in east London. The best of the boxes in the Western Region was that built at Plymouth as part of the station rebuilding and that at Old Oak Common had a similar quality although this was demolished to make way for the Eurostar

The signal box at Plymouth was rebuilt as part of the station reconstruction and opened in 1961. Designed by the BR Western Region architect's office in concrete and stone, it typified the light touch of the post-Festival of Britain architecture prior to the visually heavier approach celebrated by the later use of exposed concrete, such as that found at Birmingham New Street. (Photo: Railway Heritage Trust archive)

depot in the 1990s.

Each of the BR regions adopted their own approaches to these designs although they generally had the two-storey form with a brick-built lower level and a glazed upper level of smaller footprint capped with an oversailing roof to reduce the potential for glare from the sun. The Southern Region reverted to a very well-mannered modernist approach in boxes such as those seen on the South Western route to Exeter. The box at Winchester is a good example but it only saw six years of use before closing in 1966. For the smaller boxes of this period, a number of framed structures were built. The Western Region adopted a timber-framed, cedar-clad style of which only a handful remain, as at Evesham, although the timber-clad feature was used for the control rooms sitting atop the relay rooms below.

One of the developments of the 1960s was the integration of some of the signalling controls within station buildings such as Victoria in London and the office tower at Manchester Piccadilly: a predicament that came to seriously influence redevelopment proposals in the 1990s. The prohibitive cost of relocating this considerably influenced the design of the new concourse and its attendant facilities.

The later years of the modernization programme saw a heavier approach to the design of signal boxes. Those associated with the electrification of the eastern

route out of London perhaps represented the most coherent architectural approach. Similar in layout to the Potters Bar example but more brutalist in form with heavy rectilinear fascias and oversailing roofs following the lead set by the rebuilding of Harlow Station, the boxes at Broxbourne, Harlow Mill and Ware were amongst the best examples from the late 1950s and early 1960s. The most visually distinctive of the large boxes of the 1960s is that at Birmingham New Street. This was designed by the London Midland Region of BR and was completed in 1965. Architecturally, it should be regarded as a unique design within the catalogue of signal boxes. It is a large structure arranged on five levels and incorporates a telephone exchange as well as staff accommodation. Whilst the boxes of the 1950s and 1960s have been cited as brutalist, that epithet is more correctly reserved for the Birmingham New Street box and two other buildings in the Southern Region: the Victoria area signal box located near Clapham Junction and the London Bridge signal box located at the ends of the platform to the east of the station.

The 1970s and 1980s saw a further rationalization of the signalling network and each region developed designs for new power signal boxes. The most notable examples were at York, by the Eastern Region architects, London Bridge and Clapham (Victoria area box) by the Southern Region architects and Exeter

Birmingham New Street signal box and telephone exchange was built during the rebuilding of the station in the mid-1960s. With a different architectural team, it took on a unique design direction and remains one of the most distinctive railway buildings in the UK. (Photo: Robert Thornton)

stands foursquare and is three storeys high. It differs from the previous designs in that is formed of a concrete-framed structure clad in stove-enamelled steel panels. As with all later boxes it has limited visibility to the outside world, the internal operations mainly being dominated by the use of screens and keyboards. With Upminster, this was one of the last signal boxes to be built in the nationalized period although Upminster was never commissioned as such.

The Privatized Era

As Network Rail pushes forward with further advances in signalling and ever fewer, but more centralized, boxes the position has now been reached whereby the whole country can be operated by no more than fourteen control centres.

Whilst the modified and new control centres at Cardiff and Derby are not necessarily architecturally distinguished, the new form of design for control centre, as originally devised by Network Rail's Building Design Group, integrates all regional operating and management controls into a large, single facility. Two have already been completed and are operating at Three Bridges near Crawley, and Rugby. Another one is being built at York.

A further development with regard to the combination of train control and regional operational management is the emergence of a 'campus' to harmonize such activity, with the notion of a separate type of building for signalling purposes only now drawing to a close.

The future of the many traditional boxes that are about to become redundant is now the subject of much discussion with all those interested in the conservation and preservation of this unique asset type. Following assessment by the necessary authorities a strategy is in place to ensure that the best examples of each type can be retained for future enjoyment although this is likely to be, in nearly all instances, away from the mainline operational railway.

and Westbury by the Western Region architects. The latter was a complete break from the flat-roof forms at, say, London Bridge and Clapham in that it incorporated large pitched roofs and oriel windows, perhaps influenced by the project architect's then recent work on the neo-vernacular Hillingdon Civic Centre in a previous role.

During the late 1980s another box was added to the system following the remodelling of Liverpool Street Station. This is a complete one-off, and in a post-modern idiom. Once visible from the track, it is now subsumed into the high-rise commercial development spreading north from the station.

This box by the BR Architecture and Design Group

The Regional Operational Control Centre (ROCC) at Rugby is the latest in a line of buildings that Network Rail are constructing to replace the many traditional signal boxes across the UK. Based on a concept design by Network Rail's Architecture and Design Group this centre was delivered by contractor Morgan Sindall. (Photo: Network Rail)

Control Towers

A similar form of building was constructed in marshalling yards and the larger depots but, as the need for marshalling in the traditional manner went out of favour with the introduction of train-load freight, the need for these yards diminished. At their time and during the post-nationalized period modernization programme these towers took on a form more associated with flight-control towers. Often taller than signal boxes and with 360-degree visibility they had a distinctive architectural character that had its roots in modernism. The most distinctive were those located at the Tyne and Tees yards, but Tinsley also

BR Western Region architect's 1959 perspective of a 'model' hump-yard control building. The near building houses the hydraulic equipment that regulates the speed of the wagons being marshalled in the yard. Image: (Private collection)

had a very large framed and prefabricated structure.

Unfortunately, these no longer exist but as a form perhaps they should not be forgotten in railway architectural history, having formed part of the railway architect's workload. Even some of the smaller buildings associated with the subject of yards had a distinct character that indicated a considered design response to a functional need.

Locomotive Maintenance Facilities

Early years

When the railway companies started to switch from contract supply to the manufacture and maintenance of their own locomotive stock the need for a wide range of buildings suitable for these purposes arose.

Works and maintenance facilities tended to be quite different in their style and scale, and many locomotive-maintenance facilities were far more functionally led than the main works, which tended towards much larger, architecturally significant buildings. Local depots would at best have a building that was more in the scale of a minor-goods facility, but with satellite operations on site that demanded more basic architecture.

In the early years, locomotives were purchased from private manufacturers, built at remote manufacturing centres and transported to the railway where they would be employed. This meant that there was need for a location in which the locomotives could be assembled and then maintained for routine running and eventually, repairs. One of the most notable examples of this was that of the London & Greenwich Railway. This railway, dating from 1836, obtained its locomotives from a variety of manufacturers, some in the north-east of England and others in the south-east. The railway had a natural gateway in the form of the River Thames, so locomotives could be delivered by water to the wharf adjacent to the station at Deptford. The elevated nature of the railway on a viaduct and the access ramp that

had been constructed at Deptford gave the company the opportunity to assemble the locomotives in the arches beneath and then they were raised to track level. The station was developed to include a locomotive shed at track level as part of the building. The locomotives were of the two-axle 'Planet' class, which had been developed for the Liverpool and Manchester Railway, and their relatively light weight was no doubt an advantage when maintenance movement was concerned.

Most companies kept locomotives at strategic locations on their routes and many stations housed the local 'pilot' locomotive in a small shed, often brick-built and often identifiable by the raised clerestory roof with ventilating louvres, located along the ridge of the roof. The GWR often included a locomotive shed as part of their larger train-shed stations.

Development

The Midland Railway was one of the first companies to create a locomotive facility within a bespoke design, adopting the roundhouse design, where locomotives were housed in bays around a central turntable. A similar facility was erected by the London & Birmingham Railway at Chalk Farm in Camden, whilst the GWR erected a segmental version at St Blazey in Cornwall. The logistical benefit is obvious as locomotives in maintenance bays would not clash with access for others. The progression of locomotive storage with other companies saw a greater use of stabling sidings and that led to storage of locomotives in larger rectangular sheds, which would have been less flexible but could manage a larger number of locomotives. There is an excellent example of this illustrated by Bourne in his prints of the London & Birmingham Railway, which shows the Engine House at Chalk Farm.

The roundhouse took a number of forms as a building. The purest form was based on a circular plan accessed via a turntable as at Chalk Farm, but when locomotives became larger the turntable was positioned outside with radial tracks leading from

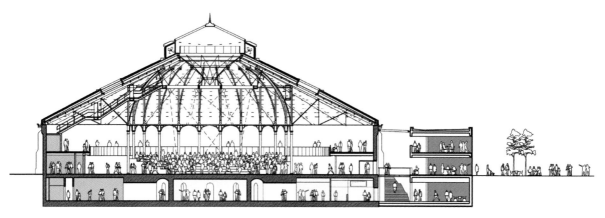

Built to house twenty-four locomotives in radial formation, the roundhouse at Chalk Farm designed by Robert Dockray and Robert Stephenson was very soon outgrown by bigger locomotives and thereafter only used as storage until the 1960s when it was 'rescued' for posterity by a group led by playwright Arnold Wesker. It is now a thriving concert venue following further restoration and remodelling by John McAslan and Partners (1997–2005). (Drawing: John McAslan)

the turntable into a building that may have only been a selected part of a quadrant. These were known as 'half round' houses and an example can still be seen in Leeds in the Wellington Quarter where it serves as a wine warehouse.

Sometimes the radial-access arrangement of tracks was housed in a square building as at Barrow Hill, Chesterfield, which has been restored as a railway locomotive heritage centre.

Throughout the middle years of the twentieth century, engine sheds became far less architectural and much more functional, with a distinctly industrial style. The longer locomotives still needed to turn but this facility was not necessarily connected so closely to the shed as in earlier generations and most sheds took on a rectilinear plan. This remained a static situation due to the privations of austerity at the end of World War II.

Changing Requirements

The change from steam locomotion to diesel meant that maintenance and repairs took on a slightly different format but generally the buildings had a similar utilitarian form. However, the introduction of diesel or electric multiple units meant that the buildings needed to be longer to be able to maintain the running set as coupled. The introduction of High-Speed Train units (HSTs) in the mid-1970s heralded a new scale of building although the architecture was usually uninteresting with a utilitarian steel-portal frame and profiled metal cladding.

The introduction of Eurostar services in the mid-1990s created an opportunity for a fresh approach to the design of the main and ancillary sheds for these very long trains and YRM were commissioned by BR to design a suite of facilities at Old Oak Common. These still stand today and are now used as a maintenance facility for the Class 800 Intercity Express Trains (IET) trains. These buildings follow the pattern of a steel-framed structure supporting a combination of insulated profiled sheeting and flat insulated panels in a well-considered arrangement. The roof structure is expressed in each gable.

Where once the physical character and needs of locomotives determined a new architectural form the sets of trains are now generally maintained in standard industrialized portal-framed sheds of no great architectural note.

Railway Hotels

The Rise of Railway Hotels

Station-related hotels form an integrated part of the character of station sites and the larger ones often dominate or obscure the outward appearance of them, particularly at the major terminals such as Charing Cross, Paddington, St Pancras and Victoria in London or Glasgow Central and Perth in Scotland.

The hotels attached to stations or located nearby were generally aimed at travellers or business users in the earlier years but the expansion of train services across the country also brought rise to the phenomenon of 'resort' hotels where hotel customers could participate in a range of activities such as tennis and golf or take advantage of the fresh air afforded by coastal resorts or inland spas.

The railways in the United Kingdom, in effect, pioneered the hotel industry as we now know it and at one stage in the early twentieth century, there were no fewer than 140 relatively substantial hotels under railway management. This represented the largest single hotel estate in railway ownership in the world at its height. Whilst not now forming part of the operational railway portfolio they are nonetheless important buildings in the social history of railway architecture and their growth was synonymous with that of railway stations during the nineteenth and early twentieth century.

Unlike other railway buildings that were designed specifically for operational railway purposes, the history of the development and management of 'railway' hotels is complicated by diverse arrangements

The Grade II listed Midland Hotel in Morecambe only had a short operational career before closure as a hotel in 1952. Designed by Oliver Hill and opened in 1933 to mixed reviews it nonetheless pioneered a new approach to the resort-hotel philosophy. The LMS and Hill were keen to utilize the best artists and craftspeople, and the original relief by Eric Gill and the mosaic by Marion Dorn are still to be seen. (Photo: Robert Thornton)

The Queens Hotel is connected to Leeds station via the north concourse, which was built at the same time as the major reconstruction of the hotel. LMS chief architect William Hamlyn designed the hotel in conjunction with consultant architect W. Curtis Green. Nine storeys high and faced in Portland stone, it commands an imposing position facing City Square and is Grade II listed. (Photo: Robert Thornton)

of ownerships and management responsibilities. Some hotels were entirely built by divisions of railway companies, some were acquired or leased from previous owners or operators and some were developed and managed by private hoteliers to take advantage of destinations on newly constructed railway lines, bringing with them, as they did, new-found custom. From being places for overnight stops between train services some became resort hotels for longer stays.

The latter were to be found at coastal resorts where hotels such as the Grand at Torquay (originally named the Great Western Hotel when it opened in 1881) were built to take advantage of a rapidly expanding market. Whilst not being owned or managed by the GWR it nevertheless was convenient for train arrivals and departures, and even had a covered walkway between its premises and the nearby station.

Railway Company Hotels

Most of the hotels that consider themselves to be railway hotels for purposes of inclusion in the railway canon of architecture came under the management of the railway companies that acquired or built them. This remained the case from the earliest known hotel built by a railway company at Euston, which opened for business in 1838, through to the nationalization of the railways in 1947 when all rail assets, including hotels, came under the control of the BTC. However, all hotels were sold to the private sector in advance of the privatization of the railway industry as a whole in 1994/7.

It is acknowledged that the first hotel in the world, designed specifically to attract railway travellers, was that built by Lord Crewe next to Crewe Station, which opened in 1837. This was then leased by the LNWR from 1864 and bought by them in 1877. However, the first hotel to be built by a railway company was the Euston Hotel located adjacent to the original Euston Station. This was designed by Philip Hardwick and opened in 1839, one year later than the station itself, which was also designed by him. Along with the Arch, these were all destroyed in 1963 to make way for the replanned and repositioned station building resulting from the electrification of the West Coast Main Line.

Philip Hardwick also designed the building forming the station entrance at Curzon Street in Birmingham at the northern end of the line from Euston, part of the upper level of which was to form hotel accommodation serving the station. The integration of hotel and station accommodation had its origins in this building, although many went to greater pains to ensure that smoke and steam from platform areas were separated as far as possible from accommodation areas. As with the Euston Hotel, the hotel at Curzon Street Station was opened for business in 1839. The main structure remains and will form part of the HS2 station proposals now in preparation.

Although there were railway company acquisitions of existing inns which pre-date the nineteenth century, the majority of hotels built for railway purposes were designed and opened for business in the nineteenth century and this is generally reflected in their classical revivalist architectural styling albeit with a pioneering use of emerging technology such as electric lighting, fire-proof construction and the use of elevators. Under railway company guardianship, a number of these were wholly modernized and updated during the twentieth century. Of this latter category there are two notable examples: the Queens Hotel at Leeds Station, which was the first hotel in Great Britain to incorporate air conditioning and central heating; and the Midland Hotel in Morecambe.

Hotel Architecture and Architects

As railway-hotel buildings generally took their design cues from the prevalent civic architecture of the period, they had more in common with major banks, company offices and town halls than the emerging field of station design: buildings to which they were sometimes attached.

As with early station designs the architects employed for hotel design were mainly drawn from established practices, many of whom were already engaged in station design. When the railway companies developed their own engineering and architectural resources, much of the later redesign and adaptation of railway hotel premises was undertaken by them, hence, for instance, the engagement of the GWR's architect, P.E. Culverhouse, in the 1930s, to remodel the Great Western Royal Hotel at Paddington. Philip Hardwick's son, P.C. Hardwick was responsible for the original design, which opened for business in 1854 along with the station it so effectively masks. The comparison in design approaches for these two elements couldn't be more different: the station pioneering the use of fine wrought-iron engineering and patent glazing, and the hotel amalgamating an eclectic mix of Renaissance and other classical revival themes, much of which was stripped away by Culverhouse.

Perhaps the most important of the early consultants in respect of their railway connections and overall railway design portfolios were G.T. Andrews who was responsible for the Paragon Station Hotel in Hull, which was opened in 1850; Decimus Burton, who was responsible for the design of the North Euston Hotel, at Fleetwood; and Francis Thompson who designed both the original station at Derby and the Midland Hotel opposite. This hotel design was intended to attract both commercial and leisure users and was planned in the country-house style.

Whilst the former Great Western Hotel in Reading has sometimes had the reputation of being the oldest 'railway' hotel still standing it has not remained in continuous use as a hotel through its lifespan. Instead

The Midland Hotel in Derby has the reputation of being the oldest railway hotel in continuous use for its original purpose. Designed by Francis Thompson, it survives opposite the location of the original main station, also by Thompson, and to which it was originally linked by a canopy and a subway. These and the original station were demolished in the 1980s to make way for the station building that is there today. (Photo: Robert Thornton)

this reputation goes to the Midland Hotel in Derby, which has an unbroken history of use.

Notable Station Hotels

Most of the major stations in the country, but particularly the termini, have notable hotels attached or immediately adjacent to them, for example, the Grosvenor Hotel at Victoria Station, London, the Great Northern Hotel in Edinburgh, the Midland Hotel in Manchester and the Grand Central Hotel at Glasgow Central. Most of these stations are contemporary with the stations they abut and are generally in the revivalist styles associated with them but there are a number of later variations.

The original Queens Hotel at Leeds opened in 1863 but was completely rebuilt in 1937 and reopened to a design by the then chief architect to the LMS, William Hamlyn, and consultant architect William Curtis Green. The building is in Portland stone in what would now be regarded as an Art Deco style but which at the time was described by *The Architect and Building News* as 'Cosmopolitan classic with a decided transatlantic bias'.

Resort Hotels

The end of the Victorian era and the beginning of the Edwardian era saw the development of some grand resort hotels, the two most notable being Turnberry in Ayrshire overlooking the Firth of Clyde and Gleneagles in central Perthshire. Turnberry was designed with 131 bedrooms and opened in 1906 to the designs of James Miller. This was regarded as one of the finest resort hotels built by the Glasgow & South Western Railway and was in a form of Arts and Crafts design similar in style to many of the large country residences of the period.

Gleneagles was conceived in the early part of the twentieth century with designs by Matthew Adams. Construction commenced in 1913 but the war years intervened, and the hotel was not completed until 1924 when it was opened by the relatively newly formed LMS.

The Midland Hotel in Morecambe was a pioneering new form of hotel building originally taking the name of what initially opened in 1848 as the North Western Hotel on a nearby site. This was renamed the Midland Hotel in 1871 but was closed in the Spring of 1933 as the LMS had a vision for a replacement that was to be on the cutting edge of modern design, making full use of British craftspeople and craftsmanship: it also pioneered the use of reinforced

A LMS postcard drawing of Turnberry Hotel, a true resort hotel devoted to those keen on golf. The seventy-eight-room hotel was designed and furnished by James Miller for the Glasgow & South Western Railway and opened in 1905. Occasionally home to the Open Golf Championship, it was sold by the British Transport Hotels group in 1982 and is Grade B listed. (Drawing: Private collection)

concrete in such buildings. Architect Oliver Hill worked with artist and sculptor Eric Gill to produce what is now recognized as an Art Deco masterpiece and which has now seen a full restoration to its original condition. The Gill elements include a low relief in Portland stone in the foyer, a ceiling feature over the circular main staircase, painted by his son-in-law, Denis Tegetmeier, and a pair of Portland-stone seahorses over the main entrance doorway. Eric Ravillious was employed to produce frescos representing morning, noon and night for the cafeteria. There is also a mosaic of a seahorse by Marion Dorn in the entrance, her original carpets having been recreated for the reception area.

It is only a relatively small hotel with forty rooms but, following restoration in 2008 by Urban Splash, it can now be seen to be one of the finest buildings of this period with its origins in the railway industry. Having been originally completed only six years before the outbreak of war, when it was taken over by the Royal Navy, it never regained its popularity, particularly as Morecambe was declining as a resort

and it was sold in 1952.

Whilst many of the station hotels were upgraded and extended in styles contemporary with their period of modernization, there was only one completely new railway company hotel building completed in the second half of the twentieth century and that is the Old Course Hotel at Saint Andrews Golf Course, which, according to Oliver Carter in his book, *British Railway Hotels*, was unflatteringly nicknamed the 'chest of drawers' following its opening owing to its design, which incorporated jutting balconies and rooms along its main elevation, its overall proportions adding to that visual imagery. This cannot be easily recognized as such as the building has now had a facelift and has been over-clad in the manner of so many twenty-first-century building makeovers. The original building was designed by the architects Curtis and Davis in 1968 and was commissioned by British Transport Hotels. In fact, it was the only complete hotel building to be constructed by them in their management of railway hotels between 1948 and 1983.

Changes of Use

Of the original 140 hotels built specifically in response to railway opportunities, only about 20 of these have been entirely demolished but a number have been closed as hotels and reconfigured to become offices or residential accommodation failing their suitability to continue in hotel use. One of the largest of these, the former North Western Hotel, with 200 bedrooms adjacent to Liverpool Lime Street Station, for instance, has now been converted into residential accommodation for John Moores University following a period of decline. The work to change its use was completed in 1977 but further restoration was completed in 2000 to provide social-function facilities and bars.

A number of the larger hotels struggled to survive during the depression of the inter-world-war period and were converted into office use, two notable examples being the Great Central Hotel in the Marylebone Road in London adjacent to Marylebone Station and the Midland Grand Hotel at St Pancras, designed by Sir George Gilbert Scott and opened in 1873.

The Great Central Hotel, designed by Sir Richard Edis and opened in 1899, was purchased for use as offices in 1945 and then became the headquarters of the newly formed British Railways Board under the BTC in 1948 where it remained in railway use until it was sold in 1986 to a private hotel chain. It is now the Landmark Hotel and is being used for the purpose it was originally designed following extensive refurbishment which focuses on the conversion of a large service courtyard into a capacious glazed central atrium.

The Midland Grand Hotel at St Pancras fell into decline as a hotel during the inter-war period and was closed in 1935 and used for offices until the mid-1980s. It is perhaps fitting that the primary occupant of this building – known as St Pancras Chambers in the BR period – was the British Transport Hotels organization, a branch of the BTC specifically set up to manage the hotel portfolio. Its fortunes were to be revived when a decision to route international train services into St Pancras was made during the 1990s and once again it could be considered for hotel use. In the event, the original building fronting the Euston Road has been converted into residential apartments by the Manhattan Loft Company, and new hotel accommodation designed by architects RHWL and

The former 200-bedroom North Western Hotel adjacent to Liverpool Lime Street Station, conceived by Alfred Waterhouse Designs in French Renaissance style, was opened in 1871. It was closed as a hotel in 1933 and was used as offices until its reincarnation as a hall of residence for students at John Moores University in 1997. It is Grade II listed. (Photo: Robert Thornton)

conservation specialists Richard Griffiths Architects has been skilfully woven into the station buildings to the west of the main shed flanking Midland Road.

There have been many proposals that didn't see the light of day including two hotels designed by Edward Lutyens in the 1930s. The first of these was at Looe for the GWR and the second was at Manchester for the Midland Railway. Percy Thomas also designed a hotel and office development at Euston for the LMS in this period, but this, too, didn't materialize due to the threat of war and the consequences of it.

One encouraging development that may set the scene for the reuse of former railway offices is the conversion of the former Great North Eastern Railway headquarters office building in Station Rise in York. The original building designed by Horace Field and William Bell (NER company architect) was much influenced by Norman Shaw and the Arts and Crafts Movement seen in Hampstead and Chiswick, and has now been converted into a first-class hotel and conference venue.

Houses, Hostels and Homes

In the days before commuting to work became an everyday practical reality, railway companies required that senior station managers needed to be located at, or close to, their place of work and many stations incorporated domestic accommodation to this end. If it could not be provided within the design of the station building itself appropriate house were often built a short walk away.

As railway companies developed and expanded it also became a necessity to provide accommodation for skilled workers close to the various works associated with, for instance, the manufacture, maintenance and repair of locomotives and rolling stock. Railway companies also endeavoured to cater for staff working away from home, particularly where driver's shifts and train timetabling meant overnight stays many miles from home towns. To this end, lodgings were often found in private premises but some of

Unlike many, the station master's house at Ribblehead Station is an independent structure and somewhat exposed to the elements. This was fully restored by the Settle and Carlisle Railway Trust and architects PPIY York in 2013. (Photo: Paul Childs)

the bigger rail companies designed and constructed purpose-built hostels for such predicaments.

A further aspect of railway employment was the care and recuperation of staff recovering from illness or bereavement: whilst the buildings used for such a purpose cannot be classified as true 'railway' buildings, those purchased for convalescence nonetheless provide an interesting dimension to the railway-estate story and duly engaged company architects in their upkeep and occasional refurbishments. In all, ten properties were purchased, each with interesting historical backgrounds. Only two of these now remain and will take in men or women needing convalescence from all industries.

Houses and Housing

In the early years of their development, railway companies bought most of their rolling stock from private suppliers but the general unreliability of such stock drove the railway companies to build maintenance and repair facilities at strategically placed positions on their networks of track. Some of the rail companies established depots and yards in existing industrial towns such as Derby, York, Doncaster and Darlington, and others were to create them on greenfield sites such as Crewe or Eastleigh, or close to existing towns or villages such as Swindon.

Where the railway works were not close to existing centres of population or where the right level of skilled labour could not be provided locally, it was necessary to provide housing to accommodate such resources and in such a way many a town area or, indeed, new town was created, the first accredited railway town being Wolverton in Buckinghamshire. This was midway between London and Birmingham and was created by the L&BR in 1838. Much of the structure of this settlement has found new uses but the historic significance of what remains is now evident.

When the railway populations grew commensurate with the expansion of the railway operations and works so too did their families and it was not unusual to see other industries co-locate in these areas to take advantage of the labour force provided by partners, wives and family members of working age. The settlement at Crewe, which grew into the town we know today, was one of the biggest railway towns in the sense that it was entirely railway-driven in scale and purpose. Under the supervision of architect John Cunningham, it was laid out in 1842 and included the provision of schools, a church and public baths, as well as other civic functions.

A typical terrace in the Swindon railway village. The first houses were complete by 1842 but the later terraces followed in stages. They are thought to be designed by Matthew Digby Wyatt who later worked with Brunel on the designs for second Paddington Station, which was opened in 1854. (Photo: Robert Thornton)

The railway village in Swindon lies immediately to the south of the line from London to Bristol, 1mi (2km) or so from the old town, and for a time it was referred to as New Swindon. The housing comprises terraces of local-limestone-built, two-storey rows set out on a small grid. The first houses were complete by 1842 but the later terraces followed in stages with 130 complete by the following year. They are thought to be designed by Matthew Digby Wyatt who later worked with Brunel on the designs for the Paddington Station we know today, which was opened in 1854. Whilst the earlier phases were built by the GWR, the later phases were constructed by private contractors. The threat of redevelopment of the site in 1960s was averted by the County Council and the buildings were refurbished and modernized.

There was a tenement block built within the area that was converted into a Wesleyan Chapel in the 1840s but there is also a large church (St Marks) forming part of the village. This was designed by George Gilbert Scott. One other building of note is the Mechanics Institute, which was built in 1844 and formed the cultural heart of the railway community, although it is sadly now in a state of disrepair.

Hostels

When the pattern of timetable rostering meant that train crews had to spend nights away from their home, lodgings had to be found near to the main loco-motive- and carriage-staging points. When services intensified and demand for accommodation grew at strategic points across railway-company routes, com-panies sometimes provided their own hostels. These were generally designed and managed by company staff and whilst they are perhaps not architecturally notable and are generally overlooked, many having been subsequently demolished, they are nonetheless part of railway-building history. Those that still exist have generally been converted for other uses. The one at Old Oak Common provided accommodation in four large interconnected blocks of two, three and four storeys in a symmetrical arrangement, now used as offices.

There appeared to be a stimulus for such a provi-sion during and after World War II when shift pat-terns were intensified and the hostels required careful management in both railway company and staff inter-ests. Some of the larger ones such as Carlisle, which

Mainly unknown as buildings in the railway catalogue, architectural care was nonetheless taken with drivers' hostels where they were purpose-built. This example at Banbury displays the Scandinavian influence of the 1950s in a more coherent way than evident at the nearby station of the same period. (Photo: Railway Heritage Trust)

could cater for more than 100 drivers had matrons and stewards. Drivers were required to provide names of home depot, times of trains worked and a time to be called when they reported in. Washing and bathing facilities were provided as were soap and towels. Some social facilities were also provided although it is not clear for how long drivers were able to take advantage of these before turning in.

Convalescence Homes

The Railway Convalescence Homes as an organization with royal patronage had its origins in 1898 and the home at Herne Bay was the first to be opened, although this closed for such purposes in the early 1970s. All in all, ten properties were acquired during the first half of the twentieth century but now only two remain for convalescence purposes at Llandudno and Dawlish.

The buildings were usually former hotels and were generally located in good positions in well-known coastal resorts. They were originally intended for use by those members of railway companies who had

been bereaved or were needing recovery from illness or injury. All of the homes were requisitioned during World War II for hospital purposes.

Formerly the Old Abbey Hotel on the east side of the peninsular, the home at Llandudno faces out across the remains of Gogarth Abbey and over the sea toward Snowdonia. This facility caters for more than 2,000 visitors annually who usually stay of one or two weeks. It was bought by BR in 1949 and closed in 2005 for refurbishment and the provision of ten extra bedrooms.

The architectural teams in the railway companies were responsible for much of the internal upgrading and alterations until the close of the nationalized period.

Goods Sheds, Warehouses and Goods Yards

The transportation of goods was the chief factor in the opening of the Stockton & Darlington Railway in 1825, and this part of the industry has been ever-present throughout the development of the railway. It

Known as the Passmore Edwards Convalescence Home for Railwaymen, the facility at Herne was built specifically for railwaymen and later railway women in 1901. As with the other homes operated for railwaymen, it was used as a military hospital during World War I. It was designed in Arts and Crafts style by Alfred Saxon Snell FRIBA. (Photo: Private collection)

brought the commercial drive to expand the railway, which resulted in the increase in passengers and the need for more stations, but it regionalized the transportation of goods and helped to develop a distribution network, which would have been unimaginable to the early pioneers. To serve this sector, facilities ranging from the simplest of goods-transfer sheds to the large distribution centres of today all form part of the history of this form of building.

Small Goods Sheds

The common element of nearly all small goods sheds was a single-sided platform, usually furnished with some form of block and tackle or crane hoist used to move goods from the wagons to a pick-up dock located in the roadside wall. Often seen as small warehouses, they were usually served by a large door or pair of doors on the roadside with a rail entrance through the gable wall, generally via a high, open arch. Invariably they had a range of often round-headed windows, typically with cast-iron frames and casements incorporating decorative multi-panes and

fanlights. The sheds were usually fitted with louvred clerestory roofs to ventilate the space with a superintendent's office located at one end of the shed. Goods sheds soon began to match the architectural style of the station, although this had not always been the case in the early years. An integrated layout can be seen in Thompson's small station and goods shed at Bodorgan on the Isle of Anglesey.

Early goods sheds are often confused with engine sheds. In many early stations, a pilot locomotive or local shunting locomotive was maintained at the station and these were housed in buildings which in the best examples matched the other buildings on the site.

The basic form of a gabled shed with repetitive window detailing became a common sight throughout the country. Architectural detailing would be restricted to contrasting materials (such as red-and-yellow brickwork), occasionally dentil courses of decorative brickwork were included and, of course, window details would reflect the style of the station or location. Later, some specific products demanded that goods sheds were provided with specific design features, especially where perishable goods were concerned, and fish docks and banana warehouses

Bodorgan Station on the former Chester & Holyhead Railway was designed by Francis Thompson. Although the goods shed on the far left is no longer in use it remains as a complete example of an integrated station arrangement. (Photo: Robert Thornton)

Thomas Brassey designed this large-goods shed located at Coleham in Shrewsbury c. 1850. (Photo: Malcolm Wood)

were included with ventilation features as part of the design. An early example exists at Coleham Depot in Shrewsbury where Thomas Brassey, engineer for the GJR, constructed a goods transfer shed for the Shrewsbury and Hereford Railway. Unusual in design in that it has two curved, arched entrance doors to the roadside, it represents an early version of the later norm.

One of the best examples of an early local goods station exists at Stroud in Gloucestershire. It is a Gothic-styled, Brunel-era structure with four-centred arched windows, built in ashlar Bath stone. It typically has a two-storey office building at one end and bears the legend 'GWR Goods Station' painted on the external wall. Redundant and vulnerable for many years, it was saved when a local preservation group decided to take it on for community use, and with grant funding from the Railway Heritage Trust made it secure and installed a power supply.

Warehouses and Goods Yards

As the commercial trade flourished by the end of the nineteenth century, local goods facilities turned into major goods distribution centres. One of the largest goods sheds is that at Llanelli in South Wales. The original goods shed at the station was a typical Brunel-era broad-gauge building, which was removed when the station was rebuilt in the 1870s. A new goods shed was built at the same time further west. An extensive structure in local stone with a slate roof, it seemed to have been given a provenance to Brunel, which clearly could not have been the case as Brunel had passed away in 1859. After falling into disrepair, it became the subject of improvement notices, but again history and local involvement brought about a change of heart. It was discovered that the goods shed was part of the location where, after serious local riots following the death of two local men, the Riot Act was read out in public for the last time in Great Britain in 1911. A local building preservation group was formed, and a future community use is being sought that will hopefully save this impressive structure and give it a future use.

In the Edwardian period, the GWR began to look at constructing larger goods facilities using modern construction methods and developed a facility at South Lambeth in London using the Hennebique ferro-concrete construction system, and then followed

Llanelli goods shed was constructed in 1878 to replace the original timber goods shed of the South Wales Railway at Llanelli. The stone replacement was quite expansive. (Photo: Paul Childs)

this with a similar facility at Canons Marsh in Bristol.

The city centre sites often contained a variety of goods sheds, some bonded, for the safe storage or onward trans-shipment of goods, ranging from the typical agricultural produce of the regions served by the railway companies to manufactured goods awaiting dispatch and distribution by train.

Whilst the goods shed was effective for the periods up to nationalization, the growth of road haulage and the demise of wagon-load freight saw a rapid decline in the use of goods sheds from the 1950s onwards and many buildings and yards became derelict or were used for other purposes. The city-centre goods-handling enterprises were often very large but relatively

The remains of the Somers Town Yard wall can be seen on Midland Road a little to the north of Phoenix Road. The Gothic-revival brick detailing closely matches that seen across the road on St Pancras Station. (Photo: Robert Thornton)

As late as the 1990s perhaps, the last goods shed to be built on the mainline network was constructed at Willesden. This was a bonded facility required in connection with the newly developed international rail links and was designed by the Architecture and Design Group of BR. (Photo: Paul Childs)

well hidden from public gaze behind high walls, the Somers Town Yard next to St Pancras being a case in point. This is now the site of the British Library and the Crick Institute, but the remains of the wall can be seen a little further north on Midland Road. The Gothic-revival brick detailing closely matches that seen across the road on St Pancras Station.

In time the local aspects of the goods shed became less significant as road motor distribution and airborne freight gave rise to a greater concentration of distribution centres, and the development of containerized transportation defined a whole new style of goods operation. By the 1960s, larger freight-marshalling yards had become a feature of the railway, such as those at Banbury where four constituent companies came together as an interchange for the freight network. Many yards were provided with control centres that developed into some modern designs, not dissimilar to airport control towers, automation being the key to the modern operation of shunting and train formation.

The widespread development of the standard transport container and the development of roll-on-roll-off ships led to a major change in the way freight was handled at port-to-railway interchanges. Large yards became the norm and sheds were replaced with stacks of containers marshalled by mobile container cranes, and the former smaller form of goods station became little more than a memory. As late as the 1990s perhaps the last goods shed to be built on the mainline network was constructed at Willesden. This was a bonded facility required in connection with the newly developed international rail links and was designed by the Architecture and Design Group in BR.

Goods yards also embraced many fine and substantial administrative buildings and those remaining are capable of making fine new social venues such as the 'Coal and Fish' offices on the banks of the Regent's Canal within the King's Cross Railway Lands, which have now reopened as restaurants.

Station Footbridges

Station footbridges are one of the defining components of the character of stations of all shapes and sizes but particularly the smaller ones found at the majority of the country's two- and four-platform through stations. Whilst they might be essentially 'engineered' components they can nonetheless be of great architectural character, particularly the earlier ones. Whilst relatively rare to find examples of those built before 1880 there are many to be found from this period onwards where railway company standard designs started to be implemented. The later plate-girder bridge took over from the earlier lattice-wrought and cast-iron models, and a variation on this is still used today.

Many of the very early, smaller bridges were open to the elements but where extended canopy protection was provided on the platforms being connected, they were generally provided with a roof and valence to match the platform canopy design. At the busier urban stations, fenestration was also incorporated. It is not clear what criteria was used for the choice as to whether to select an open or enclosed footbridge, and that debate still continues, but costs and exposure to the elements are key drivers in the decision-making.

Up until the Grouping, most of the bridges connecting just two platforms were likely to have been designed with a haunched-span section. This had the effect of reducing the length, and therefore the height, of the flight of stairs positioned in line with the platform and created an elegant span to produce an archetypical structure much in evidence on heritage railways. This arrangement, however, is providing a challenge to those who now need to provide step-free access between platforms as this stepped arrangement cannot easily be fitted with lifts to the upper level of the bridge. A further complication is also arising where the span over the track needs to be raised to allow for the introduction of overhead line equipment (OLE) above the track.

To a degree, the historic periods are characterized by the designs evident in each one, but here this is perhaps not as marked as in the main buildings.

A typical mid-Victorian, recently restored, wrought-iron, lattice footbridge at Templecombe Station. Such bridges often had the company and manufacturers insignia or logotypes cast into, or positioned in spandrel panels or brackets bracing the junctions between columns and beams. (Photo: Paul Childs)

The footbridge at Rye is typical of those made by railway companies that had their own concrete works from the 1930s onwards. Dating from 1960, this BR Southern Region example is similar to many others on the network, such as the bridge at Weeley on the BR Eastern Region that became the template for the ubiquitous Hornby Dublo station footbridge. (Photo: Malcolm Wood)

Most of the bridges of the Grouping period follow the plate-girder approach although the use of standard concrete-panel solutions was adopted widely on the LMS and SR where concrete was being used for platforms, fencing and light columns and so on. An example of the smaller bridge can be seen at Rye.

Where there was heavy parcels, goods or mail use at stations, they were usually provided with a separate bridge span with lift access but often without staircases such as those found at Worcester Shrub Hill or Macclesfield. The solution at Surbiton was a single bridge of dual height within the form of the main station building, the lower level being for passengers and the upper level being for parcels traffic. At some locations these goods bridges, being served by lifts, have created the opportunity to provide step-free access now that the goods traffic has ceased.

The modernization programme of the 1950s following nationalization saw a number of new bridge designs at stations, and perhaps those at Macclesfield and Banbury, show a direction that is still relevant. The bridge at Macclesfield is an elegant glazed structure sitting on tapered concrete supports, which gives it a lightness not seen on many bridges and its fully glazed span set a precedent for many later bridge designs. Banbury was unusual in being designed to accommodate a restaurant on the span so that passengers had a comfortable environment to wait for trains in.

Where enclosed bridges are preferred and these are fully glazed, consideration has to be given to the cleaning of the exterior. Options that have been adopted are 'tilt and turn' or inward opening windows or panels or external walkways, but safety considerations of working with water in positions above operational track, particularly where electrified, are a challenge to all available methodologies.

Where bridges of historic interest are unable to comply with contemporary requirements or standards, they have sometimes been found alternative sites. The footbridge at King's Cross, for instance, has now been found a home at Ropley on the Mid Hants Railway.

Many new footbridges have been installed in recent years, the need for step-free access being the key driver. The variety of solutions and the constraints of the various sites have led to the re-evaluation of the design opportunities, which has led Network Rail to engage with the RIBA to set up a design competition to ensure that opportunities for high design standards are optimized. This culminated in a competition and an exhibition to display the entrants at the RIBA in 2019.

An unusual level-crossing footbridge made from used and worn 'bullhead' rail adjacent to Wokingham Station. Old rail is often used for basic purposes, such as guard rails and fence posts, but nothing as adventurous as a footbridge such as this. (Photo: Paul Childs)

Railway Offices

Administrative offices have always been part of the railway portfolio of buildings but in the earlier days and before the various individual railway companies grew and took over or amalgamated with each other, extant commercial premises would have been used for this purpose. Where the opportunity arose, administrative accommodation was built into station or works premises.

Whist generally modest in scale they were sometimes nevertheless distinctive architecturally. The Bristol and Exeter building in the forecourt of Bristol Temple Meads Station is a good example.

When the railway companies grew as businesses and took on the tasks of manufacturing their own equipment and designing their infrastructure in addition to the administrative tasks of managing their passenger and goods businesses, the need for dedicated office space arose. The scale and location of such offices initially reflected the physical disposition of the activities created by each company.

The works offices with clock tower at Derby, close to the eastern side of the station, typify the proud approach to all building types serving railway functions. As with so many of the Derby railway buildings this was designed by Francis Thompson in 1840 as a single-storey building, but upper levels were added in the 1860s and 1890s. This red-brick and rusticated-ashlar stonework building is Grade II listed. (Photo: Robert Thornton)

A perspective by Lawrence Jackman depicting the new divisional works office at Shrewsbury in typical late-1950s style. Designed by the BR Western Region architect's office, it has now been over-clad in the way of so many twenty-first-century refurbishments, its clean lines having now been obscured. (Drawing: Private collection)

However, through growth and amalgamation, each of the emerging rail companies found the need to create administrative and geographical focal points or centres that are still recognizable today. This accommodation was generally distributed alongside or with appropriately located station buildings or manufacturing centres, such as at York, Darlington, Derby, Doncaster, Crewe and Glasgow, but occasionally it gave rise to the need to create individual buildings in new locations, albeit generally within city or town centres in close proximity to rail services.

The railway clearing-house building in Eversholt Street north of Euston Station is a case in point. Built in 1875 to designs by J.B. Stansby, it sits quietly in the street with no real hint that it was at one time a railway building as such, even though more than 2,500 staff were employed there.

The periodic reorganization of railway companies and functions they perform are often the spur to generating the need for offices and some of the best

What is now the Grand Hotel and Spa in York was originally built as the headquarters of the NER. It was designed by Horace Field and opened in 1906. This building and its near neighbours on both sides of the city walls illustrate the importance and influence of the railways in York. (Photo: Robert Thornton)

The Network Rail national centre building in Milton Keynes is perhaps not recognizable as a railway building as such but it reflects the values of sustainability and energy efficiency key to the future of the industry. As one of the most efficient buildings on the network, it was awarded a BREEAM Excellent rating on completion in 2011. (Photo: Network Rail)

examples resulted from such changes of administrative patterns, hence the NER building in Station Rise in York completed in 1906 and designed by William Bell and Horace Field. The later Stephenson House building in Eversholt Street in London designed by the LMS chief architect Hamlyn and completed in the 1930s was directly attributable to the post-World War I Grouping.

Whilst not regarded as distinctive, the 1950s and 1960s saw a wave of railway-office building related to major initiatives such as railway modernization. Where this involved major station work, opportunities were taken to rebuild office accommodation alongside to reflect new national-, regional- or local-level administration with the size and scale of the buildings reflecting the new management structures. New offices to meet these post-war rebuilding requirements were built across the country but were most distinctive architecturally where they were coupled with station redevelopments as at, for instance, Plymouth in the BR Western Region.

As the railway continued to readjust after nationalization, and particularly after the restructuring of the industry in the mid-1960s, a number of new administrative centres were built in readiness for major staff relocation in the early 1970s. New offices were thus built in Cardiff, Glasgow, Birmingham, York, Liverpool Street and Croydon. The York offices were demolished in early 2019 to make way for the redevelopment of the quarter of the city within the medieval walls adjacent to the original station.

Continual reorganization of regionally based staff also saw the need for smaller new area manager's office suites and the Southern Region of BR created a new form of offices known as OD70 based on the pioneering D70 station-design system.

Railway companies always favoured building their own offices and it was not until the later 1980s and into the privatized era of the 1990s that the various companies looked to provide their own space within commercial lettings, although Network Rail bucked the more recent trend and commissioned designs from GMW for its purpose-built national centre in Milton Keynes close to the station.

Railway Arches

Railway arches have traditionally been used for secondary operational activities or storage and vehicular or pedestrian thoroughfares from one side of the railway to another. In the past they have not been regarded as the best of environments. Where arches have opened onto more public thoroughfares in towns and cities opportunities have sometimes been taken to convert them into restaurants and offices so long as the difficulties of sound transmission from the trains above and the problems of rainwater leakage from track-bed drainage have been overcome.

Where a large station has been built on arches, such as at Charing Cross, Manchester Piccadilly, Leeds, Glasgow Central and London Bridge, they have usually been used to support station functions and provide vital space for train catering, station retail storage, station servicing or where convenient and commercially viable, let to private tenants.

Once hidden from the general public and the travelling passenger the arched environment is now exploited for use by them, the most recent example being the new concourse connections at London Bridge and the accommodation forming lettable retail and catering spaces along the newly restored St Thomas Street flank of the station. These have been restored to a very high standard and fully demonstrate the polychromatic brickwork so characteristic of C.H. Driver.

Railway arches south of the Thames very much dominate the urban landscape and many attempts have been made since the turn of the millennium to change the image of the environment they create,

The rebuilding of London Bridge Station with the main concourse now located at surrounding street level emphasizes the role that the arches play in the character of the station and the impact they have on the urban fabric. Imaginative reuse and skilful restoration by Grimshaw and conservation specialists Donald Insall Associates have transformed the environs of London Bridge, especially in Tooley Street and St Thomas Street. (Photo: Robert Thornton)

Not well known to the general public, the development of the canal side and the provision of a new station entrance has provided the opportunity to bring the 'Dark Arches' beneath Leeds Station into more general use. The innovative use of colour-change LED lighting together with the sound of rushing water as the River Aire passes through four of the arches is a unique experience on railway premises. (Photo: Paul Childs)

particularly where these are public thoroughfares. The most effective way of doing this has been by the use of coloured lighting and the adoption of a coloured theme for the paintable structures. A particular success in this respect has been the painting and cleaning of the Landsman viaduct structures running between London Bridge and Greenwich.

Of interest on Blackfriars Bridge Road in London are the remains of the one-time terminating station of the line into Charing Cross. The station entrance is tucked into the arches behind the bridge abutment now, but the low-relief name of the station is still displayed across the abutment, having been restored in 2006.

Hitherto unseen by the public, the arched structures beneath Leeds and Manchester Piccadilly stations have also been re-energized for public use. At Manchester the street level arches have not only been used for car parking but also form the backdrop to the taxi pick-up and short-term-parking area. Once a service yard, this facility was developed as part of the regeneration project for the station completed in advance of the Commonwealth Games in 2000. The arches beneath Leeds Station, referred to as the

Dark Arches, are an interesting feature of the station mostly unknown to the general public. However, since the interest in opening up the adjacent canal-side buildings for retail activities, the use of the arches for access purposes has grown. The interest within the arches focuses on the routing of the River Aire through four of them. There is a slight drop in level within the station footprint and the noise of the river moving swiftly through the space adds a certain drama to the site. The walkway has now been made more user-friendly by the use of dynamic, coloured LED feature lighting but the opportunities for commercial activity have yet to be fully exploited.

In the commercial areas of London and large cities such as Manchester many arches have been converted into thriving restaurants, one of the first of these being the Arch Duke in the arches adjacent to the Royal Festival Hall which opened for business in 1979. The success of this conversion pioneered other conversion of arches in similar locations.

The opportunities and potential afforded by arches in inner cities in particular for more than the traditional scrap merchants, storage or workshops, is now plain. The production of design guidance by

the landlord of the arches, which assisted in terms of essential waterproofing and maintenance access and so on, helped to realize the value of these premises. One of the gamechangers in this respect was the conversion of the arches in Wootton Street near to Waterloo Station where a group of arches were fitted out as commercial premises and marketed as such. Other successfully converted arches are located under the tracks leading to Newcastle Central Station. A number of these are occupied by architect's offices and studios.

It wasn't unusual to find railway arches bricked in and converted into homes at the lower end of the social scale. Such examples were to be seen in Limehouse and Bath. These particular examples were provided by the GWR, but generally these conversions were not built by railway companies.

Water Towers

The humble water tower is a true relic of the steam-train era and they were strategically placed around the network of stations and yards although the size varied considerably. These were generally of standard all-steel-and-iron construction of a variety of sizes to meet the demand at a particular site and its position on a given route. The water capacity ranged from approximately 2,000gal (9,000l) for a typical branch-line facility to over 200,000gal (1 million litres) on the biggest tanks serving yards and depots, which required their own dedicated water towers. The one in the former Swindon works adjacent to Bristol Street, built for firefighting purposes, was one of the tallest structures at nearly 75ft (23m) high. It was intended to provide a high-pressure supply for the nearby sawmill. Whilst the original tank has been replaced with a smaller one, the structure is still a local landmark and as a Grade II listed structure was restored in 2014.

At the bigger centres, water towers could take on a more architectural form and have lower levels constructed of masonry with accommodation within them. They were sometimes incorporated into buildings serving other functions. The Pattern Workshop in the former Swindon works is a good example; here, the water tank forms the entire roof area of the building with a tank of 240,000gal (1.1 million litres).

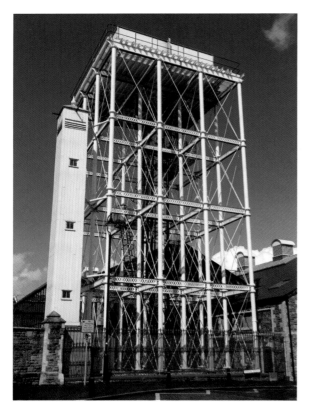

One of the tallest water towers on the former railway works at Swindon. This was located next to one of the timber workshops and storage areas, and was provided for fire extinguishing purposes rather than for steam locomotives. It is Grade II listed. (Photo: Robert Thornton)

Good remaining examples of such masonry structures can be found at Newcastle Central Station and Huddersfield Stations. Both were constructed in the stone used for the main station buildings. Such buildings, substantial in their own right, can be successfully converted into new uses should the sites be provided with suitable access as at Huddersfield. This tower was constructed by the L&NWR between 1885 and 1890. The 60,000gal (270,000l) cast-iron tank sits above a two-storey stone structure forming part of the Grade I listed station buildings. The accommodation remained in use for storage and railway operations after the decommissioning of the water tank in the 1960s but eventually fell into disuse during the 1990s. Following successful restoration it is now in thriving use as commercial office accommodation.

The water tower serving steam locomotives on the Settle and Carlisle line and located at Settle has been successfully converted into residential accommodation. Smaller than the tower at Settle, the water tower at Faversham Station has also been converted into a two-storey house. At a smaller scale, the tank at Haltwhistle Station is an attractive single-storey stone building with a symmetrical arrangement of iron-framed windows and doors, which has more

Haltwhistle water tower was built in 1861 and comprises a panelled cast-iron tank sitting atop a sandstone pump house, which more recently has been used as commercial accommodation. (Photo: Paul Childs)

The St Pancras water tower, now known as the Waterpoint, was designed by Sir George Gilbert Scott to complement the Gothic-revival station and hotel. This was relocated to its present site during the construction of the new high-speed line into the station in 2001. It is Grade II listed. (Photo: Robert Thornton)

recently lent itself to use as a cafe.

St Pancras Station was served by a 13,800gal (62,700l) tank accommodated within a neo-Gothic polychromatic brick structure designed by Sir George Gilbert Scott to match his detailing at the rest of the station. This was completed in 1871 and was located just outside the shed on the eastern side of the track where it was seen from trains in the context of the famed gasholders. The conversion of the station into the terminal for intercontinental trains necessitated the relocation of the tower and it was successfully moved in three horizontal sections to a new site 2,300ft (700m) to the north of its original site where it sits on new foundations, the original base forming part of the viaduct supporting the new tracks. The structure now forms part of the ongoing redevelopment of the King's Cross Railway Lands site and is in use as an education centre.

Water tanks were also used for other operational purposes at St Pancras and it was not widely known that the hydraulic Ransome and Napier buffers at St Pancras were once served by storage tanks hidden in the upper levels of the Grand Midland Hotel buildings.

Generally, the water tanks themselves were

A concrete-framed and panelled water tower, which was in existence at Cardiff General in the early 1930s when the station now known as Cardiff Central was reconstructed. It is listed Grade II and is seen as having group value within the context of the station. (Photo: Malcolm Wood)

constructed from segmented wrought-iron or steel panels supported on cast-iron or steel columns or masonry bases. There were, however, a number constructed in concrete although these were generally not architecturally expressive in the way that some of the larger mains water-supply tanks were, an example being located at Cardiff Station.

It is unfortunate that one of the most 'architectural' of all the water towers was demolished in the 1960s, this being the one forming the grand gateway to the Inverness train shed and through which all locomotives had to pass in order to gain entry to the shed or set off for the tasks of the day.

Memorials and Monuments

The railway industry, as one of the largest industrial sectors of the last 200 years, has not been immune to the harder side of life. During the construction of the great elements of the railway infrastructure, particularly in the earlier years, there were numerous examples of fatalities and serious injuries and often in relatively large numbers. The opening day of the Liverpool and Manchester Railway in September

1830 saw one of the most high-profile fatalities with the fatal injury sustained by the Rt Hon William Huskisson MP who was run over by the locomotive 'Rocket' at the site of Parkside Station, near Newton le Willows. A memorial tablet was erected on the lineside at the site of Parkside Station, in a classically styled structure, known as 'The Fireplace', one of the first of many railway memorials to be found on the network.

Not all memorials are placed that close to the site being commemorated. One of the most imposing is that in the churchyard of St Mary in Llanfair Pwllgwyngyll near the Britannia Bridge over the Menai Straits where a large obelisk was erected to remember those who perished during the construction of the bridge. It also includes the names of two men who died during its reconstruction in 1970. A smaller but nonetheless impressive memorial similarly located in a nearby churchyard recognizes the loss of twenty-four workers during the work to construct the Bramhope Tunnel. The memorial in Otley parish churchyard is a smaller-scale replica of the tunnel portal.

A greater number of memorials resulted from the great loss of life sustained by the industry in war. Most railway companies supplied men to the service of the

Bramhope Tunnel Memorial, Otley. The memorial, which is a scale model of the north-tunnel portal, commemorates the dozens of men who died during the construction of the 2mi- (3km-) long tunnel between 1846 and its opening in 1849. (Photo: Robert Thornton)

The NER Memorial in Station Rise, York. Unveiled in 1924 after the Grouping, this war memorial was designed by Sir Edwin Lutyens in Portland stone. The memorial inscriptions on the wing walls carry the names of the 2,236 NER employees who died in World War I, to which were added the names of those who fell in World War II. (Photo: Robert Thornton)

country, some in reserved occupations and others who enlisted. The memorials to those who gave their lives are varied, ranging from plaques dedicated to those who fell in the Boer War from the Midland Railway at Derby to the more recent plaques erected by the Railway Heritage Trust to commemorate those railwaymen awarded the Victoria Cross in World War I. Within this range there are several memorials that are designed as part of the architecture of stations, most notably that of the Victory Arch at Waterloo Station, which forms the main pedestrian entrance from the South Bank and which originally commemorated the losses of the LSWR in World War I but has been updated to reflect those losses to the Southern Railway in World War II. A smaller arch is located between the platforms and main building at Stoke-on-Trent Station to commemorate those lost in war by the NSR.

A frequent sight on stations are Rolls of Honour – usually paper memorials in frames, the most common being that of the GWR, although one of the most elaborate is that of the Taff Vale Railway, a copy of which can be seen at Cardiff Queen Street.

The memorial cenotaph at Derby was designed by Sir Edwin Lutyens as was the memorial obelisk opposite the former GER offices in York.

Located in the churchyard of St Mary in Llanfairpwllgwyngyll, the four-sided obelisk and base commemorate those who died during the construction of Robert Stephenson's tubular railway bridge over the Menai Straits prior to its opening in 1850. (Photo: Robert Thornton)

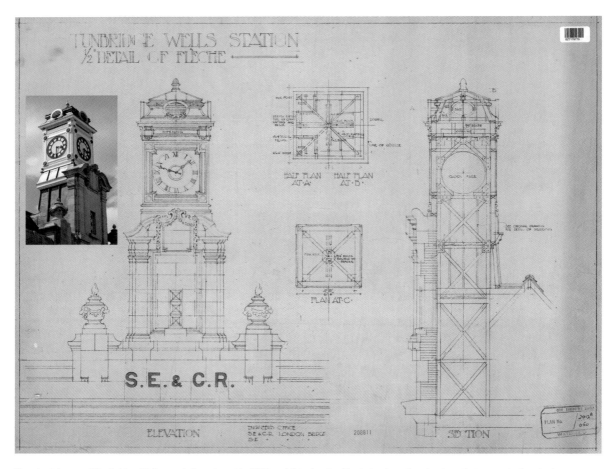

The clock tower at Tunbridge Wells was fully restored in 2019 and this drawing illustrates how the structure that supports the clock mechanism and faces is an integral part of the roof structure and the overall station composition. The restoration of the clock and tower was a category award winner for Network Rail in the 2019 National Railway Heritage Awards.. (Drawing: Network Rail Archive. Inset Photo: Robert Thornton)

Several memorials taking the form of sculptures exist, the most well known being the statue of the 'Tommy' reading a letter from home by Charles Sergeant Jagger on Platform 1 at Paddington Station. This is set in an architectural reordering of the doors and windows within the gable of the westernmost transept of the station by architect Thomas Smith Tait. The LNWR memorial designed by Reginald Wynn Owen outside London Euston Station and the South Eastern & Chatham Railway memorial at the Continental ferry terminal with bronze figures sculptured by W.C.H. King, formerly called the Dover Marine War

Memorial, are also fine examples of statuary artwork commissioned by the railway companies.

Railway Station Clocks

For those old enough, one of the abiding images of station concourses and platforms is of mechanical analogue clocks, both as an architectural feature and a once-essential source of information. The spaces beneath them became well known as places to meet and they certainly featured widely as such in films and literature.

Large clock faces also became defining features of many station exteriors as at, for instance, Nottingham and Leicester where the supporting tower is the central focus of the architectural composition. Similarly, the external clocks at London's King's Cross and St Pancras stations are an indispensable element of their respective architectural compositions and dominate the adjacent street environment.

The interiors of the large through stations, such as Perth and Carlisle, usually feature a large clock on the main departure platform but in the main termini the clock is often located in one of the shed gables as it is in Liverpool Lime Street.

Most of the older analogue clocks have had their mechanical movements removed to be replaced by electric motors but many of the significant ones have had their visible and essential mechanical elements restored. Those at stations such as Reading and Tunbridge Wells, add considerably to the quality of the urban environment as well as the amenity of the stations and are an indispensable part of a station's architectural vocabulary.

The clock on the inside gable at Liverpool Lime Street after restoration. The positions of such clocks over concourses or principal departure platforms has meant that they are commonly used as meeting places. (Photo: Robert Thornton)

Chapter Nine

Building Materials

Tradition and Change

In the UK the vast majority of railway buildings accommodating people, rather than locomotives or industrial operations, through to the later years of the twentieth century have been of traditional construction, generally utilizing load-bearing masonry. This methodology, in combination with the earlier and widespread use of cast iron, wrought iron and glass in canopy and shed roofs as at Carlisle has given many railway buildings, particularly stations, their very distinctive visual character. Without the structural capabilities of these materials, the large, clear spans and structures that characterize the great termini and bridges would not have been possible. Without the incorporation of the detailed and decorative castings that characterize so many railway buildings, this new identity would not have been possible. It is true that these materials were used to good effect in market halls, glass houses and exhibition spaces but none were so

Although the frontage building at Carlisle, built for the Lancaster & Carlisle Railway with solid 'collegiate Tudor' styling, is a tour de force from Sir William Tite, the overall station ambience has been enhanced and uplifted by the restoration of the glazed train-shed roof. (Photo: Paul Childs)

large and structurally daring or had such an impact on the general public as those devised for the railway.

Aside from the pioneering use of wrought iron and glazing combinations in large shed structures, the materials generally selected for railway structures can be seen as traditional and conservative in comparison with the other aspects of railway design such as those related to rolling stock and civil-engineering structures. The materials selected for buildings were also generally compatible with the prevailing building fashions and design idioms of the time.

There were occasionally forays into new forms of construction at various times in railway history but the only sustained periods of non-traditional construction date from the 1960s onwards where framed, panelled and offsite construction methods have generally prevailed.

There were times, however, where other techniques have been utilized such as the advanced reinforced-concrete systems used at Paddington Station in 1916, for example, the Hennebique and other ferro techniques used beneath the fourth span, the former stable block (the 'Mint Stables') and the reinforced concrete canopies at Potters Bar and Loughton in the 1950s and 1960s but these weren't widely adopted on a national basis.

Bricks and mortar are now used less with framed and panelled systems taking precedence, as in NR training schools, control centres and TOC stations such as Deptford. Traditional skills are now generally focused on domestic buildings.

There have also been times when traditional material, such as timber, has been used in adventurous fashion as, for instance, at Manchester Oxford Road Station where it was cleverly used in a conoidal-structure roof over the ticket hall and in the semi-arched platform waiting shelters, but these examples are relatively rare in the case of the concrete structures and unique in the case of the timber structure.

Where the spirit of change was prevalent in the 1960s and 1970s some materials and construction techniques, untried until then, were utilized such as glass-reinforced plastic (GRP), laminates and later

The footbridge linking the platforms at London Bridge was clad entirely in GRC prefabricated panels with integrated windows. The brown colour and heavily articulated panels led some critics to compare it to a bar of chocolate. (Photo: Private collection)

glass-reinforced cement/concrete (GRC). Standard designs for small buildings, such as lineside plant rooms and station ticket collectors' booths, became standard targets for the use of GRP although these were generally manufactured by a private company to BR specification and then delivered to site. As with all materials, the desire to use something new often outweighs the practicality of using it and it took many years to find the most appropriate uses for a material that potentially had long life and few maintenance demands.

Following post-war austerity, a number of materials options were experimented with such as enamelled metal panelling on steel frames and concrete. Wartime damage also drove repairs in materials in use in other parts of the industry, such as sections of old track, that were used to stabilize and strengthen temporary building repairs: the bomb-damaged offices and sheds at Paddington and King's Cross being two examples. Coincidentally, these sustained damage midway in their western-side (departure-side) offices.

Traditionally, most railway building materials were sourced locally or from areas served by the railway company as a matter of pride or promotion. Where necessary, materials could be selected from further afield as the transport links improved. Materials are now sourced globally from wherever they are cheapest, plentiful or most appropriate. Certainly, the vernacular element has largely disappeared from most construction except, perhaps, in the most architecturally sensitive restoration or refurbishment projects. Whilst there may be general preference for this route, the often-experienced high costs tend to favour alternative options.

A key aspect of the identity of railway buildings is not simply the function, size or even the stylistic quality of the architecture, but also the materials from which they are constructed. This can impart many messages about the building and the designer's intent and, of course, the aspirations of the company commissioning the structure. The gradual change from local or even national sources of materials to worldwide sources through the twenty-first century has not changed this dimension of a building but it has certainly eroded the sense of place that was experienced in the past and taken away the ability to 'read' it.

Stone

Stone is one of the most commonly encountered building materials in Victorian railway buildings: only surpassed by brick, which became more common as the railways expanded. Most Victorian principal civic buildings were constructed in stone, using local styles and sources, and most railway architects and engineers had extensive experience of handling it as a material. The Liverpool and Manchester Railway was fairly consistent in the use of St Bees sandstone, a deep red stone used throughout the Mersey area. The station at Edge Hill by architects Haig and Franklin was constructed of this stone in an ashlar style, with vermiculated rustic quoins.

Early railways often made use of local materials. Brunel used knapped flint and red brick quoins for the broad-gauge station at High Wycombe, which

William Tress designed Etchingham on the SER. The decorative, but heavy-looking platform canopy was added in the early Edwardian period. (Photo: Malcolm Wood)

reflected the style of many rural buildings in the Chilterns. In towns and cities, such as Bath, Bradford on Avon, Chippenham and Stroud, he retained the local style of ashlar Bath stone for the stations and viaducts and this was reflected in the more traditional style of construction.

Ashlar stone was very much part of the Gothic tradition, which was being revived during the mid-nineteenth century by the likes of Brunel, Tress, Digby Wyatt and Sancton Wood, and it is no surprise to find that their designs retain the local vernacular whether in smooth or tooled ashlar work, or rock-faced, figured, ragstone, random or coursed rubble. It appears in various forms depending on the local quarry, so it can be encountered in limestone, sandstone or as is more likely to be found in Scotland and Cornwall, granites.

Stone lends itself well to carving and decoration and, as with ecclesiastical buildings, various forms of decorative stonework can be encountered on the railway. Both Gothic and classical styles are executed with detailed carvings including rusticated and vermiculated quoins, string courses, column capitals and other functional and purely decorative details.

By the early twentieth century, Portland stone was being favoured for the grander stations, particularly those with large office ranges and hotels such as Victoria and Paddington. It was also used later at the Queens Hotel in Leeds. Generally encountered in ashlar form, it can also be decorated with impressive sculptural work.

Brick

The expansion of the railway, particularly in urban areas, began to dictate the use of more economical materials. This led to a widespread increase in the use of brick as a material of choice.

The early railway in London depended on the availability of bricks to construct the viaducts necessary to carry the railway across changes of level and particular ground conditions. This was certainly the case with the London & Greenwich Railway, which used expansive quantities of Sittingbourne stock bricks at a time when London was being heavily developed and the demand for bricks was particularly high. Many new brickworks were established to meet railway

The recently restored station frontage at Snodland is a good example of 'tuck' pointing, once widespread, but now not often encountered. (Photo: Paul Childs)

West Hampstead Station by Landholt Brown enjoys a position on a tree-lined street with a coloured, facetted and illuminated glazed-brick wall lining the main approach route. (Photo: Peter Cook(

demand, taking advantage of the existing canal and expanding railway networks for distribution.

Brickwork was widely used and in a simple monochrome form with buildings depending largely on the design of fenestration and roof details to impart design quality. It was sometimes embellished with stone string-course detailing, and the works of C.H. Driver are probably the most notable examples of this form of detailing. As with other architects of the period, he was also an exponent of polychromatic brickwork, combining red, white and black bricks in window and door heads and other elements as a foil to the body of the buildings, generally constructed in yellow stock. He also made use of specialist 'tuck' pointing whereby brickwork was given the pattern of white course and perpend joints by application of a white mortar.

One material allied to the use of brickwork and found at the end of the nineteenth and beginning of the twentieth centuries was terracotta and its close relation, faience. Being a glazed, moulded product, it could be produced in a variety of contrasting colours as in the lettering for Culverhouse's GWR structures of the 1930s, the Art Nouveau graphics on the frontage of Leicester Station and the frontage of Kettering Station by Trubshaw.

Terracotta blocks could be used in conjunction with brickwork to give contrasting textures and because terracotta was essentially a moulded ceramic, quite complex design features could be incorporated. Nottingham and Leicester stations by Charles Trubshaw are good examples, as are the remaining platform buildings at Pontypridd.

Glazed bricks rather than ceramic tiles have also been used in areas subject to very heavy usage, and can usually be found in nineteenth-century subways. However, perhaps the most successful use in recent years has been the construction of a long boundary wall at West Hampstead Station. Here, faceted, glazed bricks in shades of green and yellow have been used to create a wall that cannot easily be defaced by graffiti or fly-posting. With its concealed illumination, it provides a safe and welcoming approach to the station.

The station at Helmsdale dates from 1870 and was built for the Duke of Sutherland's Railway (later the Highland Railway). It is a rare example of the use of shuttered slip-form concrete, a forerunner of the construction method used for tower-block lift shafts today. The system, known as Drake's Patent System, typifies the adventurous nature of the Victorian engineers and builders who were keen to encompass new techniques. (Photo: Paul Childs)

Concrete

Concrete is often regarded as a structural material and is generally covered over but on the railway estate it can sometimes be found being used in innovative ways. The station at Helmsdale in Scotland, although looking at first glance to be a traditional, rendered, cottage-style building is, in fact, constructed of poured concrete using the Drake Patent System. This is a forerunner of the slip-form of concrete construction used to create concrete lift cores in modern high-rise buildings.

Concrete also appears in the works of the GWR in the 1920s when the French, Hennebique ferro-concrete system was used for the construction of the goods-handling facilities at Canon's Marsh in Bristol and South Lambeth in London (now sadly demolished) and the extensions to Paddington Station beneath the fourth span. The use of this reinforced concrete system at goods depots enabled larger spans to be constructed and reflected the increased importance of freight to the railway system. It was a marked change from the older goods stations, which were large, expansive buildings generally constructed in brick with steel-trussed roofs. The development of concrete construction also enabled the SR to create the International and Moderne-style stations at

Surbiton, Southampton and other locations in the 1930s.

Good examples of the use of ferro-concrete panels and structures can be found in the former SR stations of the inter-war years where the use of a kit of parts with interlocking posts and panels was quite widespread, especially in the south-western area.

During World War II, concrete was invaluable in its use in the structural elements of bomb-proofed signal boxes, such as the surviving example from the LMS at Runcorn and indeed many lineside buildings. It was also used in association with heavy reinforcement to produce semi-subterranean control centres, an example of which still exists at Newport in South Wales.

In the 1950s, several stations were reconstructed in concrete, such as BR Western Region's Banbury Station, where the whole station was subject to the designer's pen, even down to the waiting-room furniture. BR's modernization programme of the 1950s and 1960s led to many station reconstructions, the most notable of which was perhaps Coventry. It was designed by the London Midland regional architect's office, to what were then outstanding contemporary standards incorporating large areas of glazing and emphasizing the horizontal roof planes. It has been described as brutalist, but that is an unfair description

The connection between the Underground station and the main concourse at London Bridge is a mixture of quadripartite brick vaults and shuttered concrete vaults taking on the same form but clearly expressing the new intervention. (Photo: Paul Childs)

of what was a key element of the post-war regeneration of the heavily bombed city of Coventry.

Used expressively, concrete found its use in a number of other buildings in the 1950s and 1960s, most noticeably in the Birmingham New Street telephone exchange and signal box structure and, slightly later, in the two signal boxes at London Bridge and Clapham. Perhaps its most widespread visible use in smaller buildings was in the CLASP system utilized by the Southern Region for a number of stations. A good example of its use is also to be found at the Derby Rail Technical Centre completed in 1966 and soon after bestowed with a Civic Trust Award. It is now a private business park.

More recently, exemplary use of concrete can be seen in the 1990s Lawn rebuilding at Paddington Station where pre-cast units were used for the exposed balcony floor structures and more recently as board-shuttered in situ forms creating quadripartite vaults in the arches beneath London Bridge Station, both by Grimshaw.

Both the SR and the LMS had concrete plants where they made sectionalized footbridges, lineside huts, platform-support trestles, fence panels, platform coping stones, and so on. The concrete footbridges on the SR and LNER became the templates for the cast-metal Hornby Dublo train sets of the 1940s, 1950s and 1960s.

Some buildings constructed in masonry were given added protection by the use of cement render or stucco finishes. These are usually found on classically detailed structures but can become a regional or local vernacular, as with 'harling' in Scotland where surfaces are rendered, but quoins, window surrounds, and so on, may be exposed to give contrasting detail.

Timber

Timber was extensively used in the early years of the railway to construct shelters and smaller buildings, including stations, and later as a staple material for many signal boxes and goods sheds. It also found favour for the construction of over-track train sheds, such as Frome on the GWR, the heavy detailing of the structure contrasting with the lighter metal and timber composite structures used elsewhere.

The GWR used timber in early station construction,

The GWR's constituent company, the Oxford, Worcester & Wolverhampton Railway, opened the timber-chalet station at Charlbury in 1853. It is a rare survivor of a Brunel chalet design executed in timber. (Photo: Malcolm Wood)

particularly on the Cornwall Railway. Elsewhere it was used for small stations in an Italianate chalet style, Charlbury Station in Oxfordshire being the sole survivor.

The Midland Railway also used timber in the construction of some of its earlier platform buildings, usually allied to cast-iron and steel-framed structures, whereby the timber enclosures were constructed within the skeleton of the canopy structure. Kettering platform buildings are a good surviving example of this form of construction, whilst there are still examples of boarded station buildings such as at

Manchester Oxford Road Station is a complete one-off, designed within the BR (LMR) offices during the late 1950s. Opened in 1960, it required major refurbishment in the 1990s. The structural principles inherent in the design of the main building were supplemented by additional reinforcement which allowed the overall form to remain as built. (Photo: Robert Thornton)

Wateringbury in Kent, and Cambrian examples such as at Newtown in mid-Wales.

Broad vertical-panel timber fencing has been used for platforms countrywide in recent years, but the Midland Railway used characteristic diagonal-timber fencing from their early history, and this is still valid today as an effective, modern style of fencing.

Laminated timber was used to great visual and structural effect at Manchester Oxford Road, which was opened in 1960. Its light weight and ability to be detailed to suit an unusual site configuration inspired a genuinely unique solution and building form. Whilst widely admired now, this was never to be repeated and demonstrates the freedom that many railway architects felt able to express within the architectural direction and spirit of their respective offices.

Iron and Steel

Iron has had a great impact on the design and character of railway buildings. Its use from the early days of the railway was key in enabling the engineers of the day to create innovative and awe-inspiring structures to carry the railway over previously unbreachable obstructions.

Whilst wrought iron was favoured for structures such as box-section bridges and large-span roof structures in the early days, its limitations in workability and strength saw steel take over and its use was then limited to more decorative elements and repetitive components such as railings, although many wrought-iron structures remain in place as at Paddington and St Pancras.

Cast iron can be seen on virtually every Victorian

The visual impact of the use of iron and steel in railway structures can be seen to no better effect than in the great train sheds, particularly the curved sheds at Newcastle and York. However, the large flat spans such as Carlisle, Bournemouth and here at Perth are also powerful. The stone building is by Sir William Tite and dates from 1848. The large-scale ridge-and-furrow roof is by Blyth and Cunningham in 1885. The building is Grade B listed. (Photo: Paul Childs)

The cast-iron waiting room at Worcester Shrub Hill Station, believed to have been constructed around 1862 was the work of the nearby Vulcan Ironworks. The infill of glazed majolica tiles was the work of Maw & Company of Broseley. The structure is a unique survivor on the railway network. (Photo: Malcolm Wood)

station platform as part of the platform canopy or main-shed support system. Recognizable in the shape of ornate columns and decorative spandrels, it was also used for rainwater goods, decorative friezes and roof crestings (especially at the hands of designers such as John Taylor and C.H. Driver) and on many elements of platform furniture such as lamp columns, fences, seat frames and urinals. Some particularly elegant metal fencing can be found in both wrought and cast iron. Many examples and variations exist across the country. Surplus railway materials, such as expired rail, can also be utilized to add further interest.

The most decorative use of cast iron can be found on the 'Up' platform at Worcester Shrub Hill Station in the form of a tile-clad waiting room. Constructed for the Hereford & Worcester Railway around 1862, it is not clear whether the structure was intended as a demonstration piece for exhibition at trade shows or as a marketing tool for the GWR, but it clearly was a later addition to the station. The cast-iron framework by the local Vulcan Iron Works and the infill of colourful and decorative majolica tiles by the Maw Company of Broseley are a sheer delight, and the building has recently been restored and brought back into use.

As for a number of small building types, the Edwardian, GWR, corrugated-iron pagoda-style waiting shelter was used at Denham Golf Club Station. It is part of a group listing. (Photo: Malcolm Wood)

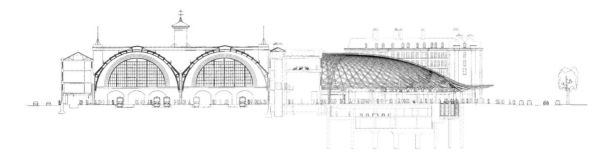

The diagrid roof structure at King's Cross served the functional purpose of spanning a complex array of structures and impediments out of sight beneath the concourse level and providing a clear circulation space connecting and unifying two hitherto poorly connected arrays of terminating platforms. (Drawing: John McAslan and Partners)

Corrugated iron was widely used for railway buildings for a variety of purposes, ranging from roof coverings, fencing panels, and for smaller lineside buildings, particularly lamp rooms, huts for fog signalmen and refuge buildings for track-maintenance teams working in remote areas. The GWR also used corrugated iron for a series of utility buildings in the early Edwardian period when there was an expansion of the metropolitan railway network around London. These were designed in a style called the 'pagoda' due to the use of a curved eaves detail reminiscent of Chinese pagodas.

Rainwater goods, such as gutters and downpipes on early railway buildings, were generally of cast iron, with various sizes and configurations for gutters in ogee, half-round and square profiles, and downpipes in square or round sections. This principle continued right through the nineteenth century and well into the twentieth century, until there was a move to use drawn metal profiles, which gave lighter, thinner, metal sections but enabled a wider variety of profiles to be produced and reduced the number of joints required in the system with consequential reductions in the risk of leaking joints damaging the external surfaces of buildings. Cast aluminum is now a good alternative to cast iron where replacement historic gutter profiles are required. It is lightweight and is appropriate where canopies are involved.

The expressive use of iron and steel faded with the closure of the Victorian period but was resurrected again in the 1960s with the advent of hi-tech. On the railways, this found its place in the new concept of station building adopted by the BR Eastern, London Midland and Southern Regions, which comprised glazed modular structures with exposed lattice-steel beams and flexible interiors. This was extended to small office structures in the 1970s but perhaps the most prominent station examples are found at Bedford and Gatwick, and later at Reading station where the 1989 roof is partly constructed of a nodal-space frame.

A proprietary 'space deck' solution also found its place in the temporary concourse structure fronting King's Cross Station in the early 1970s and, more extensively, over the forecourt at London Bridge Station a few years later.

However, the most expressive use of a steel-roof structure from the nationalized period was to emerge in the early 1990s at Waterloo Station when Nicholas Grimshaw and Partners together with YRM Anthony Hunt designed the sinuous tapering roof form over the new international platforms at Waterloo Station. Grimshaw went on to design a new roof structure over the Lawn at Paddington, thus opening up views into the middle span of Brunel's tripartite roof structure. The diagrid roof structure over the concourse at King's Cross and the three dimensionally curved roof structures over the concourse and platforms at Manchester Victoria are two of the most visible and innovative solutions to large-span steel structures on the railway network.

Roofing Materials

In the railway environment, these can generally be split by three kinds of application: smaller 'traditional' roofs, larger roofs on train sheds or industrial buildings and canopy roofs. Occasionally, the small-scale applications cross over and are utilized on large-scale projects such as the slated roof at St Pancras. Generally, however, the larger, pitched and particularly barrel roofs utilize membranes or sheet materials such as corrugated iron or, more latterly, profiled aluminium.

Welsh slate was widely used during the Victorian and Edwardian eras although clay tiles found favour as the local vernacular in the south and east. These can be found in a variety of styles from a plain rectangular format to interlocking Roman style. They lend themselves to combinations of irregular shapes such as the decorative roofs at Stoke-on-Trent. Decorative ridge crestings and finials, in clay or fired earthenware, are also common features.

John Taylor, who designed many stations for the London, Chatham & Dover Railway, developed a clay, interlocking bridging tile that he used on several railway buildings in the south-east. Early roofing on lineside and station buildings sometimes included the use of zinc slates, which were favoured on the GWR for the Italianate chalet designs.

Sheet materials, particularly corrugated iron, have been used on the railways for building purposes from the 1850s although it is said that there was competition for its supply from project demands in the Crimea. The material was particularly favoured on the GWR as a roofing material at stations, such as the second Paddington, constructed in 1852, and on the through-train shed at Frome. It was also a small-building cladding material as used at stations such as Denham Golf Club, which is one of the aforementioned pagoda buildings.

The roof cladding at Paddington has been replaced on a number of occasions since the original construction but always in metal sheeting of approximately the same profile as originally specified by Brunel. In more recent replacements the profile close to the valleys between the vaults has been altered to allow for a larger gutter and a syphonic drainage system. (Photo: Robert Thornton)

Paddington roof has been replaced five times since the original sheeting was removed in the early twentieth century but each time with a profile and colour match as close to the understanding of the original colour as possible. The later replacement materials for corrugated iron have been of coated steel and the most recent was coated aluminium.

In the more industrial environments such as depots and train sheds, particularly large-goods sheds, steel-framed buildings and readily available sheet materials gradually replaced brick structures in the inter-war years. Profiled asbestos sheeting became relatively commonplace until the inherent dangers of the material were more clearly articulated. From the 1960s onwards, sheet cladding materials were constructed of plastic-coated metals although these would rust where trimmed or damaged. Aluminium gradually took over but was more expensive than the ferrous metal options. A fashionable option in the 1960s was for the profiled sheets to be curved. This allowed designers to eradicate the junction of roof and wall, and to locate the gutters at ground level to ease ongoing maintenance and avoid unnecessary excursions to roof level. The single-thickness sheets utilized in earlier decades required additional insulation to render the internal spaces habitable but the later cladding sheets generally incorporated it to meet contemporary standards.

Whilst rolled lead and zinc sheeting were traditionally favoured materials for low-pitched roofs and mansard roofs, the vogue for flat roofs during the 1930s led to the use of mastic asphalt or bituminous felt, which required 'hot work' to install. These solutions are almost always difficult to repair and unless failures are addressed promptly the inevitable ingress of water can cause long-term damage.

Bituminous felt was used at times on some lightweight timber buildings, and a good example of this is the small terminal building at Pwllheli on the Cambrian Line in Wales. Single- and multi-ply polymer membranes with welded junctions are now preferred for lightweight flat roofs. In combination with metal flashings, these give high-performance solutions and, by using appropriate colours, a good representation of original materials such as lead or zinc can be achieved. Blackburn Station was treated in this manner as part of the 1980s Railtrack Backlog Maintenance Programme.

There aren't many railway buildings with traditional ridge-and-furrow glazing but St Pancras in London has faithfully recreated the form of glazing originally used there, having for many years been fitted with a form of GRP sheeting, which had discoloured badly with the effects of diesel exhaust and UV light. (Photo: Robert Thornton)

Glass and Glazing

Glass has been used as a roofing material over platforms since the earliest days of passenger railways, mainly as a result of the influence of Joseph Paxton and his use of a system of glazing design for the Great Exhibition in Hyde Park of 1851. Stations built after 1851 widely adopted this method including King's Cross Station (completed in 1852) and the second Paddington Station (built in 1854). As with the Great Exhibition halls, standardized glass sheets were held in patented metal frames. All evidence of this form of glazing has now been removed from Paddington during various phases of re-roofing and to allow for the construction of the Crossrail Station on this site.

Early glazing appeared in a cast form, but the risk associated with it being unreinforced led to the development of Georgian wired glass, identifiable by the 'graph paper' appearance of the wires within the glass, which might be 'rough' cast or smooth in finish. Corrosion in the wires, particularly where cut and exposed to the elements, can, however, lead to stress cracking.

Translucent sheet materials such as fibreglass or polycarbonate, have been extensively used to replace ageing glass, particularly patent glazing in canopy and shed roofs. Whilst early hopes for this material encouraged its use, the effects of UV light and the tendency to attract diesel fumes and other environmental pollution common around stations such as brake dust, contributed to serious discolouration. Whist most has now been removed from the system, it remains to be seen on the area of Liverpool Street Station roof that was not renewed in the rebuilding programme of the 1980s/90s. The advantage of this over-glass was that it could be laid as sheets without the need for the sub-framing systems required by patent glazing. It was also 'unbreakable' and therefore safer in respect of maintenance access and inspection. Should the material not have discoloured it is possible that it would have been looked at more favourably today especially as it imposed less strain on the overall roof structure by virtue of its light weight. The polycarbonates now used can replicate the traditional appearance of rough-cast Georgian wired glass even to the extent of having photo-etched

Most of the large areas of glazing on station roofs have been refurbished during a wave of building improvement projects. Stations, such as Lewes and more recently Stirling, have taken advantage of lightweight polycarbonate glazing to create roofs of traditional appearance whilst significantly reducing the load on the structures. (Photo: Robert Thornton)

An aerial view of the ETFE roof over the angled concourse and platforms within Manchester Victoria Station. The springing point of the supporting ribs is on the near side and allows for an uninterrupted connection to the existing station buildings with the flexible nature of the ETFE allowing seamless transition around the curve. (Photo: Martine Hamilton Knight/Building Design Partnership)

reinforcing wires imprinted on the surface. A good example of this recent use is on the glazed platform canopies and roof sections at Lewes Station.

The rough-cast surface, whether glass or poly-carbonate, appears to offer a much better solution to overhead glazing than clear glass. Clear glass allows views through to external features on adjacent buildings that might not necessarily be attractive, for example, the backs of the adjacent buildings with all the attendant down pipes, soil pipes and ill-con-sidered flues, ventilation extracts that can't be seen from the street side. Rough-cast glass also diffuses light in an attractive way and allows the form of the roof to be clearly defined. An exception is St Pancras, where the Barlow train-shed roof is so much higher than surrounding buildings that the clear glass only allows visibility of the sky, which can be seen in all its meteorological moods and impacts on the internal environment in an interesting way.

The use of toughened and laminated glass requires heavier frames, and these are not always support-able by historic, lighter-weight structures without further reinforcement. Other systems have been used, including planar- or patch-fixing systems such as those adopted at Manchester Piccadilly during the shed-roof restoration works in the late 1990s.

A new type of glazing has been used since the late 1990s on station roofs and that is ETFE (Ethylene Tetra Fluoro Ethylene). This was first used on the platform roof at Blackburn and was then used on a larger scale over the concourse at Manchester Picca-dilly in 2001. Its light weight and durability allowed a much lighter support structure to be used with all the economies that that brought about. It was used as a temporary sheet covering at Edinburgh Waverley until the shed roof could be re-glazed traditionally, and more latterly at Reading Station where it is used in the new canopied areas. Its most expressive recent use is at Birmingham New Street and Manchester Victoria Station where its intrinsic characteristics have allowed it to be utilized for the sweeping, three-dimensional curves of the new concourse roofs.

The Midland Railway was one of several companies to use bespoke metal-window designs in the 1870s. These lozenge windows were supplied by Richards of Leicester, who also produced cast-iron columns and spandrels. (Photo: Paul Childs)

Window Framing

One of the key features of railway buildings is the variety of window and door styles that architects have included over the years. The traditional designs used on Gothic and Tudor-styled buildings often contrast with the sash windows and multi-pane windows found elsewhere. Fortunately, many of the early styles constructed in timber have been retained and that has also been the case with metal-framed windows often found in the locomotive and goods sheds, and the lozenge-paned windows by Richards of Leicester, often found in Midland Railway structures. The 1930s saw widespread use of metal-framed Crittall-style windows with their fine glazing beads, which are an inherent part of the International style.

Recent years have seen an increase in replacement of modern materials such as powder-coated aluminium and uPVC, largely based on maintenance requirements. Many multi-paned signal-box windows were replaced with large-format uPVC windows during the early 2000s, as signal-box environments were upgraded. Of course, new builds in the current

era, with requirements for improved environmental performance have produced a new regime of design, which in time will define this period of construction. A relatively early, but generally unnoticed, employment of uPVC window framing was on the Bristol and Exeter station offices at Bristol Temple Meads.

Doors on many stations were generally framed and panelled, and of elegant proportions until the advent of standardized solid-core flush doors from the 1960s onwards. Many of the earlier doors have survived, but as mobility access requirements have become more prevalent the heavier doors have often been replaced by lightweight doors, often glazed with powered opening systems.

Floor and Wall Finishes

The selection of surfaces, throughout stations in particular, has a major impact on the perception of the quality of the premises. For instance, in respect of flooring, the gradual switch-over from asphalt surfaces in the larger station premises to lighter-coloured surfaces, such as terrazzo (most major stations), limestone (Paddington) and porcelain (Manchester Piccadilly platforms), from the 1980s onwards made a vast difference to the appearance of those stations and changed patterns of cleanliness and maintenance.

Selection of appropriate floor surfacing is now one of the major design considerations in the progress of a project with a complex array of selection parameters based on performance requirements such as slip resistance, initial cost, strength, durability, maintenance cost, replacement availability, cleaning requirements and, of course, appearance.

From the outset, the finishes of platforms have been key to safe access to trains. Early platform construction methods relied on either skeletal timber-trestle structures or masonry construction with infill, which was often no more than compacted cinder. Eventually brick pavers were used, and whilst this gave a robust surface, any movement in the basic construction would result in uneven surfaces. Copings to the trackside edge were often carried out using blue engineering bull-nosed coping bricks. Some early platforms used large York stone slabs, which, whilst having a high-quality appearance, had risks of cracking attached, especially as the weight of wheeled barrows gradually increased. Whilst the early cinder-platform surfaces allowed gradual drainage, the adoption of mastic asphalt, tarmacadam or impervious slab finishes meant that gradients and falls were necessary to allow surfaces to drain freely. Some railway companies adopted a fall away from buildings towards the track but as platform edge heights increased over time and safety standards developed, the resultant fall away from the platform edge towards the station buildings led to the inclusion of drainage runs.

During the 1930s, timber trestle-platform construction gave way to a precast-concrete trestle system known as the 'harp' form of construction, named after the form of the cross-platform supports. These were topped with concrete-slab panels, which again required the addition of a non-slip surface usually mastic asphalt with a 'crimped' effect.

The standard for platform design is now well established with concrete coping and tactile warning surfaces to assist the visually impaired. There has also been a return to some of the forms of surfacing used in earlier times but brought up to date with clay and concrete pavers and high-quality stone finishes at significant stations.

Floor and Wall Tiling

Ceramic tiles have been used extensively as a wall or floor finish on railway buildings, particularly in bars, refreshment rooms, waiting rooms and other areas subject to heavy usage such as circulation routes and toilets. They have occasionally been used in semi-outdoor spaces too and perhaps the best example of this is in the waiting rooms at Worcester Station described earlier where heavy-glazed majolica tiles and unglazed, biscuit-surfaced, encaustic or through-coloured tiles can be seen.

At Nottingham, the Arts and Crafts finish in some of the platform buildings from 1903 are executed in Burmantoft glazed tiles with earthy browns and golden yellows included. The style of heavy-glazed tiles lends itself well to the inclusion of figured detailing. At the other end of the scale, ceramic tiling was also prominent as a means of applying detail in the 1930s, with the former ticket office at Taunton being a good example of tiling in a domestic style. In the modern era, ceramic tiling became a standard for any internal areas where maintaining a clean interior was important.

Latterly, 'rainscreen' panelling has been popular. This can be either in metal, timber or, as in the case of new station buildings at Nuneaton, in ceramic tiling. This style also appeared in large format as part of the Network Rail modular station design. In some areas slate and granite panels have been used.

The interiors of the buffets located in the platform buildings at Nottingham are fine examples of the use of glazed tiles from the Burmantoft Company. (Photo: Paul Childs)

Glass-Reinforced Cements and Plastics (GRC AND GRP)

These materials have been in use since the 1960s on railway buildings but have never become mainstream.

Some standardization has been possible, and designs have been produced for small buildings such as ticket collectors' booths, lineside plant rooms and even footbridges, the latter being of interest because of its light weight.

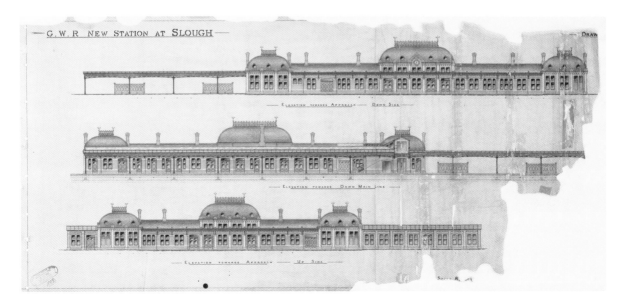

The zinc fish-scale roof tiles on Slough Station roof were replaced with GRC tiles cast from the mould of the originals in the early 1980s. This roof was listed Grade II in 1984. (Drawing: Network Rail archive)

The largest buildings to make use of GRC were the former BR computer centre in Nottingham where it was used as a repeatable cladding panel and the former footbridge at London Bridge where it was used as cladding. Such was its ability to be moulded to intricate patterns that it was used as a replacement material for the zinc fish-scale roof tiles at Slough Station in the early 1980s.

The relatively maintenance-free and durable nature of GRC has led it to be used for inaccessible building components such as replicas of timber-canopy valences, particularly where these oversail the platform edge as at Basingstoke. It can faithfully replicate the intricate profiling of individual pieces of timber in a long construction component. GRC also lent itself to the replication of dormer-window framing on an earlier restoration of St Pancras Chambers. Cladding panels in the form of 'shiplap' timbers have even been used for traditional signal boxes.

The most surprising early use of GRP was in the late 1960s in the historically sensitive Paddington Station where the platform ticket barriers, ticket office and travel-centre frontages were constructed of GRP panelling. The latter was removed in the late 1980s to allow a reconstruction of the familiar Platform 1 arched façade and a new barrier-line construction with new indicator board.

Chapter Ten

Style and Identity

Railway Building Identity

The individual buildings within the railway portfolio share many architectural attributes with many other contemporary buildings. However, it is generally their response to specific railway functions and the combination of siting with other operational elements that helps to determine their identity. Key signage and visible branding are obvious methods of identifying a station but it is more difficult to identify without closer scrutiny the many railway buildings that have fallen out of operational use and where there is no visible evidence of railway lines or other operational paraphernalia.

Much has been written by architectural historians about the styles of architecture adopted by railway architects and engineers, but it is quite difficult to identify the logic of the choices made, particularly where genuinely new and perhaps unique forms of architecture were adopted. Perhaps there should be a clear distinction made between the purely engineering form of architecture present in the great sheds, which, whilst not having precedents did have the ability to inspire awe and wonder in observers, and the purely architectural forms of other elements of railway buildings, which had more to do with civic associations of power, wealth and social acceptability.

However, styles of decoration, use of materials,

This Cheshire Lines Committee station at Cressington, designed to reflect local urban villas, deals well with the constraints of access into a cutting. (Photo: Malcolm Wood)

juxtaposition of building elements and certain features in combination do create buildings with an unmistakable overall identity. Even the humble boundary fence can have an important part to play in the architectural identity of railway buildings as they often express particular regional and company characteristics.

The styles adopted in the nineteenth century such as Gothic, classical, baroque and even cottage orné and so on (which Caroll Meeks in his book *The Railroad Station* refers to as picturesque eclecticism), for railway buildings were perhaps understandable, bearing in mind that these were already familiar in domestic and civic architecture in the UK and likely to be accepted by landowners and public authorities alike.

It would be interesting to know though what the train companies were thinking of when their architects were designing stations in the 1930s (Luton), 1940s and 1950s (Manchester Oxford Road) or even the 1960s when there were no real or tangible precedents for such structures or, if there were, these were not necessarily thought to be wholly appropriate to the railway environment.

Whilst not picturesque, railway architecture has certainly remained eclectic throughout the twentieth and twenty-first centuries so far with no signs of ever becoming unified in style save for the opportunities offered by individual programmes such as Crossrail or HS2 but, even there, individual stations are being designed by individual groups of architects with their own design philosophies and drawing on their own favoured sources for inspiration. In each

of these cases, the thread that will draw individual sites together into a harmonious whole will be the strength of the applied 'branding' and such elements as the signage systems, the design of common operational equipment and, indeed, the trains that connect the stations.

The history of railway design in the second half of the twentieth century saw a move towards standardization at a national level where possible. The standards adopted by the Big Four grouped companies for common elements such as footbridges, trackside buildings and fencing, found their way into the nationalized industry post-1947 and many of those were in use throughout this period and up to the 1994 privatization. Where possible, standards merged or were combined to encourage economies of scale from a purchasing and maintenance point of perspective. The BR corporate identity programme contributed to this too with certain elements of station paraphernalia forming key components in a manual aimed at visually unifying the entire mainline railway system, embracing all station signage, seating, clocks and staff uniforms as well as rolling-stock liveries and other forms of branding.

Decoration

It was possibly the opportunities provided by the use of cast iron in buildings that drove further forays into decorative railway architecture in the nineteenth century and that, in turn, gave identity to the railway architecture of the period. Each architect, engineer and railway company had the opportunity to generate unique moulds and patterns that could be used for building components such as columns, brackets, spandrels and other very visible roofing components. Column bases, shafts and capitals were often the focus of decorative expression and many railway companies had a pattern for line-of-route stations but then adopted an individual style for their termini or large stations, particularly where they required platform-base columns such as York, Newcastle Central, Glasgow Central, Manchester Piccadilly and Edinburgh Waverley.

Most of the Victorian castings were from pattern books and were further adapted by the introduction of company emblems but there were some pioneering new approaches. The original column capitals used at Paddington Station were, for instance, designed to tie in with the style that Digby Wyatt adopted for the other decorative work at Paddington, particularly the roof ribs and wrought-iron arabesques in the span gables, which were restored and reinstated as part of the station improvement works undertaken in the late 1990s. The column capitals that are in place now are 1980s cast-aluminium replacements for the failed cast-iron capitals of the same design introduced in 1929 when the original capitals and columns were themselves replaced as part of a major roof-repair programme. A faceted column and capital design were then chosen to replace the circular section elements originally designed for the station. A further unique application of decorative metalwork can be found at Great Malvern Station where the column capitals, whilst very attractive in their own right, are, in fact, constructed from formed sheet metal rather than cast iron.

In the period leading up to Grouping, the practice of using cast iron for structural and decorative purposes had virtually ceased and structures such as canopy frames and columns were constructed of steel, usually in an economic and utilitarian fashion still to be seen at places like Westbury and Newbury

The cast-iron capitals within the historic train shed at Manchester Piccadilly were selected from a palette devised by the Railtrack Property Major Stations architecture team, which allowed colour and tonal variations within themes. However, this wasn't to be repeated, analysis of historic colours being the preferred route. (Drawing: Robert Thornton)

stations on the former GWR.

With the passing of the Victorian and Edwardian eras, the use of elaborate decoration on buildings, for example, polychromatic, articulated brickwork, passed out of fashion on railway buildings, as it did on architecture generally, and never really surfaced again on contemporary buildings in a form that was familiar. Even where elements of decorative architecture appeared in later eras, for example, during 1920s/30s Art Deco or 1970s/80s Postmodern, the railways adopted these embellishments in a very limited number of buildings where they were generally applied or integrated as set pieces, such as cartouches or panels, rather than embraced within the core construction.

It is true that identifiable and expressive styles of building have evolved but apart from the integration

The former LMS headquarters building in Eversholt Street, London, was opened in 1934 and designed by their chief assistant architect, W. Hamlyn, and consultant Albert Heal incorporated. Virtually out of sight, a Portland stone relief depicts the LMS Wyvern and a form of winged carriage on tracks. (Photo: Robert Thornton)

of reliefs, set pieces of sculpture or specifically designed fixtures and fittings, the buildings themselves are generally devoid of 'decoration' as it was known in the earlier periods.

Even where opportunities might have presented themselves in the later postmodern period, there are no good representative examples of that idiom on the operational railway, although the 'air rights' building straddling Charing Cross Station is an unabashed structure by one of the genre's main proponents, Terry Farrell and partners (*see* Marcus Binney's book, *Palace on the River*).

Perhaps the most recent example of a decorative approach rather than an expressive approach is to be seen at London's Liverpool Street Station where BR's Architecture and Design Group under the guiding hands of Nick Derbyshire and Alastair Lansley created balconies, walkways and concourse accommodation in what they described as an anthropomorphic style. They also incorporated many new elements that borrowed the decorative inspiration and style of the original building, for instance, the cartouches on the entrance structures and the recreation of No. 1 Liverpool Street.

During this same period this team were designing new stations at Woolwich Arsenal and for the new Eurostar services at Ashford International, which incorporated stylistic elements developed in the new work on Liverpool Street whilst also paying reference to the 1930s Holden stations for the London Underground.

Colour

There are two main considerations in respect of colour on buildings: a) the inherent colour of the main building materials and its constituent parts, and b) the applied colour that can vary over time and is usually applied to components rather than the main building, although in the case of stuccoed buildings this can apply to the main structure also. The colour selected

The Sir George Gilbert Scott former hotel building fronting St Pancras is a tour de force of red brickwork originally sourced from Edward Gripper's works in the East Midlands. Whilst the adjacent Somers Town Yard structures have been demolished, the British Library pays homage to its neighbour in respect of the colour of the brick chosen for its construction. St Pancras was Grade I listed in 1967. (Photo: Robert Thornton)

in either case is an important factor in the architectural appreciation of the whole, and in particular in respect of its identity. The colours inherent in the strong red brick and terracotta buildings, such as those stations at Leicester, Nottingham and London St Pancras, are key to their character. St Pancras' colour would have been all the more powerful and pertinent if it had still been adjacent to the former

The stations and structures on the Settle & Carlisle Railway enjoy a consistent paint palette across their portfolio and a conservation guidance document ensures its accurate application. (Photo: Paul Childs)

Somers Town Goods Yard, which shared its choice of brick and Gothic detailing with the great station building, both completely oblivious to the yellow stock bricks all around.

Applied Colour

The application of colour in a station environment, which often embraced much ironwork, has always helped to determine the quality of the overall building to which it is applied. However, more latterly perhaps it may be seen more as a means of illustrating an operating company's identity and has sometimes been applied without thought to its overall impact, which is often detrimental.

Throughout railway history, companies have applied colour to building components to display their identity but perhaps it wasn't until the advent of red lamp posts following the launch of Network SouthEast in 1985 that the general travelling public were abruptly reminded that branding on the railways played an important part of the service they were taking advantage of.

Previous generations of train companies were generally keen to have visual consistency across their own estates and many produced painting schedules for their maintenance staff to adopt as and when the need for repainting arose although this may not have been to the same high standard that the Settle and Carlisle stations from Hellifield to Appleby enjoy now.

Historic Use of Colour

Much research has been carried out into original colour schemes for railway buildings, particularly stations, and these have been reused with the comfort that the building now looks as originally intended even if not wholly to twenty-first-century taste and sensibilities. However, this has sometimes been done without recognizing that today's architectural sensibilities are different to those of previous eras.

Research often shows that colour schemes have changed many times in the history of a building and when selecting colours during, for instance, a restoration project it is not simply a matter of going back to the original, which might have had important milestones subsequent to its opening. There is also sometimes a difference between evidence found at a site and authenticated written references. In site research undertaken at Paddington Station in the 1980s, with the assistance of English Heritage, a very early paint application revealed that some of the original ironwork was unexpectedly painted a bright salmon pink although contemporary documented reference material indicated the use of greys and terracotta. This latter documented selection formed the basis of the 1960s roof restoration following the World War II overpainting of the entire structure in a cream colour. It was also adopted but modified slightly during the restorations of the 1960s, 1970s and 1990s.

There is often no clear evidence about original colour schemes for buildings and even where there is some written guidance, until the advent of standardized colours under the British Standards, names and descriptions of colours could mean different things to different people. Paints were often mixed in company depots rather than by independent suppliers and as a result hues, tones and colours could vary from one batch to another, certainly from one site to another. Hence the 'stone' colours adopted by the Great Western schemes could vary significantly, for instance, from Paddington to Penzance. The colours adopted at Moor Street were based on site research and, whilst they have become widely adopted as an attractive scheme, there is not necessarily the historic evidence to support their use 'ad lib'.

Railway Company Approaches to Colour

The Major Stations group in the early privatized era prepared colour advice for each of the major stations based on architectural sensitivities but using the adopted dark green of the Railtrack corporate palette where appropriate. This was used at both Edinburgh Waverley and Glasgow Central successfully and remains to this day. The palette was developed further and became more flexible in order to reflect the architectural context or established historic precedent. For the restoration work at Manchester Piccadilly a colour palette was established by the in-house team, having taken a cue from a system used by Danish State Railways (DSB). Whilst successful in its implementation, this was not used again. During the late 1990s, a Major Station palette of neutral greys and creams together with a signature colour was used at each of the major stations when they came to be repainted although there is no such philosophy now and schemes are generally discussed and approved with local planning authorities and other stakeholders where buildings are listed or in conservation areas.

It is perhaps interesting to note that on most Continental railway systems, colour is not generally used to accentuate structures in the way that seems to be commonplace here. SNCF in France tend to use a traditional 'verdigris' colour and DB in Germany tend to go for greys.

Where building paint is used as a mechanism for company branding it is often problematical in that the colours are generally better suited to graphics, publications and other forms of identity and weren't devised with buildings in mind. It is rare to find the two suited. A further issue is that because the railway estate is leased, following the 1994 privatization, with different maintenance responsibilities falling across landlord and tenant, the branding via painting can only be applied to the element of the station that the TOC has responsibility for. In many stations this has meant that branded colour schemes sit alongside whatever colour scheme the landlord has inherited or adopted and not always satisfactorily. This is noticeable at places like Darlington where the columns are in the TOC colours, but the roof is a combination of older BR and Railtrack selected colours.

Over the last twenty years, or since the major station refurbishment work of the 1990s was undertaken, most architecturally significant or important stations have adopted colour palettes that satisfy most users and authorities, particularly if the stations are listed and where the colour palette was approved in consultation with the authorities.

Historically layered paint colours on buildings can reveal a lot about their history and their analysis can enable us to see the buildings differently. The original paint colours revealed on the Barlow shed at St Pancras Station were unexpected and for some perhaps difficult to accept as entirely appropriate in the twenty-first century but who would now regret the adoption of the light blue for all the cast- and wrought-iron work in the shed roof.

There was a vogue in the 1980s for community-based projects to support the repainting of large railway artefacts, such as bridges and stations, where these had a visual impact on their neighbourhoods. The more successful of these schemes limited their palettes and used subdued colours that would stand the test of time but some of the palettes chosen have passed their prime, physically and fashionably and now, unfortunately, look tawdry. Paint fades over time and colour-matching from site can therefore be difficult and can lead to inappropriate colours being selected unless the fading process can be taken into account.

Signs and Signage

Signs and signage have always played a part in the architectural character of the more public-facing railway buildings, particularly stations. In the earlier periods the emphasis was on labelling facilities such as waiting rooms and toilets, and so on, rather than the more typical and extensive wayfinding seen today. This is possibly because station layouts were generally simpler, with even big stations, such as King's Cross and Paddington, only relying on a single departure and a single arrivals platform and a logical sequence from the station entry point to the departure platform.

Each railway company had its own style of script for such purposes but in essence they were very

Two station signs from different railway eras, the upper being the restored nineteenth century 'running in' sign at Malvern Link, and the lower from the nationalized period, where regional colours were adopted by British Railways for signage prior to the rollout of the later corporate identity in the 1960s. (Photos: top, Robert Thornton; bottom, Malcolm Wood)

similar. It wasn't until the Grouping period that the notion of company-brand style was introduced and each of what became known as the Big Four designed a corporate logotype and a suite of letter forms that had multiple purposes. This effort was limited in application as the concentration of brand and image was generally directed towards trains, promotional literature and other graphic uses.

The nationalization of the railways in 1948 was to see the BTC take on a corporate logotype and introduce a common letter type for station names and signage, the names being a white font on a regional background colour: green for the Southern

Region, blue for the Eastern Region, orange for the North Eastern Region, carmine red for the London Midland Region and Scottish Region, and brown for the Western Region.

It wasn't until 1965 that, following the Beeching report in 1963, the constituent parts of the BTC were restructured and the railway elements were rebranded as BR with a new and comprehensive corporate-identity package applicable to all aspects of train design, graphic applications and station signage in a package designed by the Design Research Unit (DRU). Contrary to popular belief, the identity programme did not apply itself to buildings except where signage was applied, although it did apply itself reasonably well to the rectilinear modular buildings of the period. The application of the corporate identity continued until privatization. Thereafter, the development of business sectors saw interpretations of it, as well as the creation of sector logotypes and certain types of branding.

The logotype had come to express more strongly than any other sign or symbol the location and identity of a station. The symbol, now 'owned' by the Department for Transport and known as the National Rail symbol, was originally designed by Gerry Barney of the DRU and its use is obligatory at all stations, having become so comprehensively associated with station locations.

Railtrack took the initiative to redesign all the signage related to the stations under its control and again engaged the DRU to undertake the work adopted latest experience from other European railway systems, which favoured a white letterform on a dark blue background. The original BR corporate standard formed a base for this exercise, but the new font was carefully designed to be more computer-friendly and was named 'Brunel'. Lloyd Northover had been employed to devise a station-branding package for each major station and an element of this in the form of a coloured band was incorporated into the bottom of each key sign. Later modifications and updates by were undertaken in 2010 by Steer Davies & Gleave. Each of the train operating companies have produced signage and branding standards for use across their own portfolio of stations and operational premises.

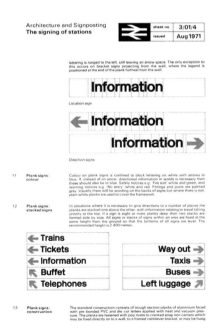

The BR corporate identity programme, launched in 1965, created a new universal signage and branding package to be used for all buildings and graphics. The image on the left illustrates the fonts and sample 'pictograms'. Following the 1994 privatization, the evidence of this on stations has all but disappeared. Railtrack, and later Network Rail, created their own signage for their stations in white on blue font, in line with international practice. (Image: Henning Ltd/Department for Transport, left; Network Rail right)

Chapter Eleven

Building Features and Design Considerations

I N ADDITION TO THE NATURE AND FORM OF the core building elements, railway buildings take their architectural character from a number of aspects pertaining to their function and use, particularly stations. The physical configuration and assembly of elements, such as platform canopies, buffer stops, footbridges and signage, together with the raft of operational equipment all contribute to the unique identity of a given station. The following section highlights some of the key elements of railway buildings and the design influences that shaped them.

Porte-cochères

The transfer of passengers to station buildings from road-going vehicles often takes place under attached canopied areas, which in the bigger stations may have been, or may still be, within or alongside the train-shed areas as at, for instance, London Paddington, Liverpool Lime Street, Edinburgh Waverley or London Waterloo. However, in some notable instances, this feature of a protected entrance has been adapted from a Renaissance model in the form of a porte-cochère, which has the secondary architectural purpose of providing a grand statement

Newcastle Station has the grandest porte-cochère on any station building in the UK. Added as a later element to the station building, it perhaps lost its original character when an upper level was added in the 1950s. Now fully enclosed to designs by Ryder Architecture, the Porte-cochère is protected from the elements as part of a wider traffic management plan. However, its status as a porte-cochère has been diminished although its external appearance remains powerful.

Built in 1899 for the Great Central Railway, the iron-framed porte-cochère with moulded zinc details links Marylebone Station with the former Great Central Hotel, now known as the Landmark and once used as the headquarters of the British Railways Board. (Photo: Malcolm Wood)

and significant character to the main entrance of a station building.

Porte-cochères were formerly used to protect carriages and their passengers whilst transferring the vehicle from a driveway or carriageway into a courtyard. They also provided protective cover for passengers at the main or secondary entrances to buildings of importance. This feature inevitably found a use at railway stations, most famously at Thomas Prosser's Newcastle Central Station but also at other significant stations such as York, Nottingham, Leicester, Brighton and London Marylebone. The latter was possibly the last of the genre to be built at a mainline station in 1899 and possibly the only one to serve a dual purpose: facilitating covered transfer of passengers to the station whilst simultaneously providing a covered walkway between the station and the adjacent former Great Central Hotel, now the Landmark. Other notable examples can be seen at Glasgow Central and London Victoria.

Initially these were designed to protect the relatively well-heeled arriving by carriage but have now become the major taxi pick-up and set-down locations for most stations. They generally consist of a patent glazed roof and supporting structure of cast-iron columns or masonry colonnading as at Leicester, Nottingham or York. The glazed roof of the grandest example at Newcastle was removed when the

additional storey of railway-office accommodation was incorporated into the structure in the 1950s.

Of the wholly iron and glass structures, Marylebone is one of the boldest and most notable, comprising distinctive sections and gables over the pavement, the carriageway and the hotel entrance. Of the smaller provincial stations, Worcester Shrub Hill is one of the best examples of its type. Its symmetrically positioned structure at the head of the approach ramps indicates the importance attached to this architectural element even though it is a lightweight and relatively small structure. It comprises a patent glazed roof supported by slender cast-iron columns fringed at the eaves with cast-iron lotus leaves and timber valancing similar to that found on the platform canopies. Other notable examples of this genre can be found at Glasgow Central, Hove and indeed Brighton.

Some early examples of this building element have been removed as at Great Malvern and London King's Cross, but there are examples where redundancy has led to reuse. At St Pancras this feature has now become the roof to a top-class restaurant. Whilst not in themselves necessarily of the highest architectural merit – Newcastle aside – they nonetheless provide a significantly practical element to a station design and, indeed, add a certain gravitas and character to its architecture.

Canopies and Valances

One of the most distinctive features of many of the medium-sized and larger stations is the platform canopy. These are so distinctive, in fact, that in many instances it is possible to identify the railway company that built them from their form or from their detailing.

Functionally, they are there to protect passengers from the elements whilst waiting for, boarding and alighting trains, but they also originally served the purpose of protecting goods and equipment stocked or temporarily stored on platforms prior to loading. These vary in size and coverage considerably from small porches, verandas and cantilevered roof sections through to fully glazed awnings or semi-independent structures such as the magnificent structure at Wemyss Bay and the less well-known Stirling.

Platform Protection

All of these were generally designed to protect the numbers of people expected to be waiting for trains at any one time in relation to the service frequency at a particular station. At the smaller and earlier stations, the external canopied area was often designed into the station building as a roofed area even where the main building was two storeys as at, for instance, Ellesmere Port or Box Hill & Westhumble. The GWR took a slightly different approach on its single-storey buildings by projecting the roof itself over the platforms.

The most common form of station canopy is probably the cantilevered form with support being provided by the station building and, depending on the projected cantilever, a row of columns. As it has always been the British practice to set these back from the platform, a further cantilevered section is then provided to form protection to the train side.

The method of pitching the roof so as to facilitate rainwater drainage varies but the most usual, and most problematic from a maintenance point of view, is to slope the pitch towards the track and position the gutter on the leading edge and, where this is a double-pitch roof, to position a valley gutter between the canopy and building. The regular maintenance of both building and canopy is essential to preserve the integrity and condition of both structures but the ongoing difficulty of doing this has led to many premature failures of the buildings and the canopies to which they are attached.

The gutters positioned over the platform edges are particularly difficult to get to without affecting train services and, where these are electrified with overhead equipment, the proximity means that isolations, and thus interruptions to train services, are needed to facilitate repair and cleaning. There are many instances where failure to do this has led to the timber valences beneath the gutter falling into serious disrepair and then being removed or cut back.

The traditional approach to canopy design is typified at Torquay with standard GWR cast-iron elements such as columns and brackets. The platforms here are wide enough to warrant glazing adjacent to the buildings. (Photo: Robert Thornton)

The rebuilding of Plymouth Station pioneered a new vision of glazed canopies for the BR Western Region with a structure-free soffit: all necessary support being out of sight, above the glass. (Photo: Railway Heritage Trust)

The same operational conditions also prevent regular painting and cleaning.

These problems were well recognized after periods of low maintenance such as during and after World War II. Where new canopies were required, a new approach to their design was trialled, most notably at Plymouth where an inverted form was designed to drain rainwater to a gutter above the columns centrally placed on the platforms. In this instance, the roof structure was provided above the glazing, thus providing an uninterrupted glazed soffit. Similar structures were provided at Port Talbot and, whilst overcoming the main maintenance problems, these were not without their own maintenance requirements particular in respect of glass cleaning.

Where canopies are not that deep front to back there is no real need to provide glazing, although the dappled light through the traditional rough-cast glass has always provided an appealing visual environment. The decision has been made in many recent projects to dispense with the glazing and the new canopies at stations, such as Reading and London Bridge have adopted this approach. The cutbacks and clearance from operational elements over the track, the need to take rainwater away from a position over the platform edge and the need to reduce the cleaning of glass have all led to the architectural form adopted at these stations.

Valances

One of the most characteristic and significant elements of a station building is the design of the timber valancing that often adorns the leading edges of canopy roofs. This feature sometimes extends to the gables and eaves of other roofs such as those over porches, footbridges and trans-shipment-building loading bays.

Much has been said about their distinctive design, which often relates to a specific railway company but not a lot has been said about their purpose or the derivation of their design. Yes, the designs are often attractive and there is an evident desire on behalf of the designer to be different, but there is also a practical purpose in their form of construction.

Valances were generally provided for additional weather protection to those people boarding or alighting trains or for those handling the trans-shipment of goods from train to depot or vice versa. However, it should be noted that at the time they were built they were more often than not constructed to over-sail the train so long as the lower edge was not foul of the loading gauge of the train. However, with the advent of overhead electrification to power trains, the physical clearances required to operate safely means that this type of canopy design can no longer

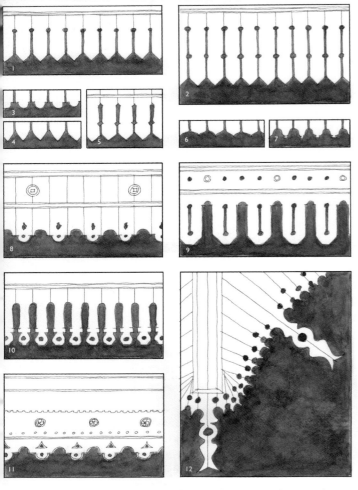

There are many variations of valance design across the network. Examples 1–7 illustrate the most common forms together with variations of lower profile. Examples 8–12 illustrate rarer forms at (clockwise from 8) Rye, York, Liverpool Street, Sheffield and Stirling. (Drawing: Robert Thornton)

together with the dagger-shaped bottom element are a good way to visually mask variations in level whilst also, importantly, allowing the valance to follow any curvature of the platform below, whatever its radius and without the visual faceting that would inevitably occur if longer lengths were to be used horizontally. It was also more economic to use shorter lengths of timber that could more easily be replaced when needed. The various forms of profiling adopted by contractors would also have helped to conceal any variation between each piece when affixed and could also absorb any discrepancy caused by natural movement, shrinkage, deformation and so on, over time.

As already pointed out, one of the shortfalls of the traditional canopy design is the positioning of the rainwater gutters and downpipes, which, if left blocked can cause rapid deterioration of the timber valances. Having recognized that this feature adds a disproportionate amount of character to a station it is often necessary to find suitable alternatives that retain the visual qualities without incurring the same maintenance liabilities. A number of solutions have been tried including fret-cut panels adopting the same profiles and GRP or GRC mouldings. These allow for speedier construction and are generally maintenance-free thereafter.

Restaurants, Bars and Buffets

The railway restaurant and refreshment facility has been the subject of nearly 165 years of railway humour, ever since Brunel commented on the state of the food available at Swindon Station on one of his journeys whilst building the GWR between London and Bristol.

The ongoing reputation has been difficult to dispel but there is now an appreciation that some of the accompanying architecture deserves greater exposure. The view is finally giving way as many of the older premises have been reinvigorated and, in many cases, wonderfully restored architecturally although many intervening 'improvements' have made this difficult,

be implemented without re-profiling the canopy structure, as was the case, for instance, at Paddington Station, when the first electrified trains were introduced in 1997. They can thus still be present but in cutting them back they no longer afford the protection they once did.

The vertically slatted form of their assembly is a practical way of addressing the difficulties of maintaining a level and true parallel line to the platform below. Achieving this with horizontal lengths of timber that would maintain their consistent appearance over a longer period of time would be difficult, particularly where sections needed to be abutted, joined or lapped. The vertical joints and the patterned profile

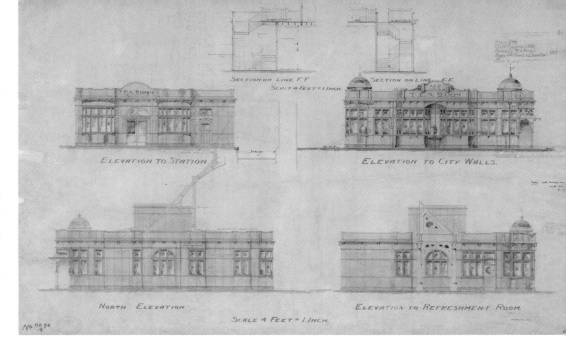

The tea rooms at York Station are an interesting variation on the more usual facilities within the main station buildings. Following many years of use as a model-railway display, the tea rooms are once again a refreshment facility following sensitive restoration. (Drawing: Network Rail archive)

ELEVATION TO STATION

SECTION ON LINE F.F.
SCALE 4 FEET = 1 INCH.

ELEVATION TO CITY WALLS.

SECTION ON LINE E.E.

NORTH ELEVATION

ELEVATION TO REFRESHMENT ROOM.

SCALE 4 FEET = 1 INCH.

particularly where major service routes have been hidden behind wall panels and suspended ceilings.

For many years and prior to the provision of restaurant cars and refreshment facilities on trains, passengers in need of personal breaks and refreshments had to avail themselves of facilities at stations en route. It is not surprising that these stops saw frantic activity and that the architectural niceties of the facilities themselves may have been overlooked by the fleeting user.

Where usage of refreshment rooms might be a little more relaxed at, for instance, large terminating stations, the facilities might have been a little better acknowledged but continually changing fashions and styles of dining made the underlying qualities of these facilities difficult to appreciate. The post-World War II period saw the biggest changes to these facilities, when in an endeavour to shed the universal image depicted in well-known black-and-white films of the period, all historic features were generally covered up. Of particular note was the tendency to lower the ceilings to make the spaces more intimate

Originally the First Class waiting room, the Centurion Bar at Newcastle Station is a spectacular example of the high Victorian art of colourful ceramic tiling. Whilst hidden for many years this restored example is one of the best on the railway network. (Photo: Paul Childs)

Each era commands its own architectural styling and this new facility at Plymouth typifies the approach of the early fifties. However, nearly every other example of this period has been swept away. (Photo: Railway Heritage Trust)

whilst simultaneously allowing the introduction of air-handling plants and other services. Ironically, this development generally prevented further irreversible alteration to the walls and ceiling features above these levels and, when revealed, gave plenty of clues as to how future restoration should be carried out. The large dining rooms at St Pancras and Waterloo are good examples of this practice but one of the best examples of this is the Centurion Bar at Newcastle Central where the original tiles were revealed in all their glory in 2015.

The restaurant facilities at stations in the earlier days were generally managed by private individuals in premises leased to them by railway companies but by the Grouping and certainly into the nationalized period they were generally managed by the rail companies. During the nationalized period and into privatization they were managed by both railway companies and private suppliers under agreement.

The 1950s, 1960s and 1970s often saw attempts to introduce radical cover-ups to traditional interiors but most of these have themselves been stripped out subsequently, either because the designs became out of date or simply did not last the course in terms of wear and tear. Examples of pop-art interior design flourished for a short while at Paddington and Birmingham New Street, but these have long since gone. An attempt to provide a modern restaurant at

Euston was reasonably well received but its enclosure behind glazed screens was felt to be deterring potential custom. This was removed simultaneously with the desire to create an older pub image once more as 1960s modern went out of fashion. This wish to turn clocks back a bit saw the end of the brightly coloured laminates at Paddington too.

Entrepreneurs have seen the value of the character that the quality of original railway premises can add to their business and successful restorations have taken place at Sheffield, York, Birmingham Moor Street and Huddersfield. The bars in these stations have created unique facilities that have gained their character from the strength of the original railway-company interior designs. Of particular note is usually the decorative tilework on walls and floors.

On a smaller scale, the growth of the letting of smaller-scale accommodation at stations since around 2010 has allowed businesses to take advantage of local demand generated by proximity to cycle routes or other leisure activities such as the cafes at Yatton or Worcester Foregate Street.

Retail and Advertising

Like all subject matter related to railway specialisms, railway retailing and commercial advertising could form the subject of a much larger discourse. However, it is important to recognize that the most successful results architecturally are those where consideration of the potential is explored at the early design stage. This must be factored into the design, particularly where retail potential drives passenger movements as this could affect a station's core operational performance. It is now recognized that commercial retail provision and the potential for a station to become a destination in the community are not mutually exclusive.

Station retail has changed out of all recognition from the earlier days of railway travel. It has nearly always been present from the earliest days of specialisms such newsagents and tobacconists, although these prevailed until well into the 1980s. A much greater variety of offers for travellers took root across stations nationally when a separate 'Station Trading' division of the BR Property Board was established. The impact of this change was immediate, and stations have subsequently changed visually and operationally, particularly at the bigger termini.

Stations were often characterized by the inclusion of free-standing kiosks but most of these have long since gone. They were generally of wooden construction and designed to be located against walls, sometimes single-sided but occasionally serving customers from three sides. Where these kiosks backed onto accommodation there was sometimes an option to turn the kiosk into a walk-in unit as on Platform 1 at Paddington. There are very few of these kiosks remaining on the mainline system although they are to be seen on some of the heritage railways such as Loughborough Central. Stations provided the biggest business for a number of well-known retailers, especially John Menzies and W.H. Smith.

W.H. Smith opened its first station bookstall at Euston on 1st November 1848, having seen

The latest example of a high-quality station retail environment is to be found at St Pancras, where only the highest level of detailed design and fit-out is permitted. Architects Chapman Taylor were engaged for the retail and commercial aspects of this design. Rigorous standards of control are applied in order to maintain this quality. (Photo: Robert Thornton)

the potential of selling newspapers and books on a nationally connected transport system with a ready-made customer base. They had spotted that train travel facilitated the reading of newspapers and books in a relatively comfortable environment. In Scotland, another nationally known name, John Menzies, opened its first railway bookstall in 1848 and negotiated its first bookstall in Edinburgh Waverley in 1862. These two companies dominated the newspaper stands and bookstalls at stations for well over 100 years.

It probably wasn't until the 1970s and 1980s that the opportunity for railway companies to create income-generating retail really expanded and that may have been related to the freeing up of space at stations following a reduction in traditional operating activities and methodologies.

Good examples of retail projects that have been carefully integrated into the historic stations are to be found at Glasgow Central, where an entire building was created by the BR Scottish Region's architects to match the famous teak 'torpedo' buildings; St Pancras's former undercroft; the island building at Victoria, which is integrated into the wall dividing the Brighton side and Kent side of the station; and amongst many more the rebuilding of the Lawn at Paddington Station. All of these have set relevant standards for future reference, but one of the most important is now the restoration of the arches, both internal and outward facing, at London Bridge, which are now being revealed following the full opening of the reconfigured station in 2018.

The quality of retail architecture on stations varies but one of the best contextual examples is at Glasgow Central where the details and form of the famous teak concourse buildings were replicated in the 1980s to form additional retailing and refreshment facilities. (Photo: Paul Childs)

It is hoped that the overall impression of railway buildings, particularly stations, is of an architecturally interesting, generally well-maintained infrastructure. Of course, there are poor examples but if one compares images of, for instance, the major stations struggling through the 1950s, 1960s and 1970s to the same examples seen now, the comparison is startling. The current administrative and organizational context and structure of Britain's railway system is reflected in the eclectic mix of railway architecture seen now. In many ways, this is akin to the early Victorian era before a recognizable national network was established. The wheel has turned full circle in this respect: there is no national identity for the system and not even a commonly used signage system that might unify the travel experience, as advocated in the Government's *Better Stations* report of 2009.

The sale of former railway assets, such as hotels, and the privatization of the railways has meant that many buildings such as those related to train production, rolling-stock maintenance and rail-company administration are no longer regarded as railway buildings. This generally leaves stations as the face of railway architecture today. As such, the recognition of the part they now play, and indeed the part they have played in the past, has elevated their status in society as hubs of movement and community.

There is no doubt that the railway industry has seen a massive transformation of its building stock in terms of condition, quality and functionality since the latter years of the nationalized railway. This has not happened by accident. The industry, since the later years of the 1970s, has endeavoured to improve the lot of passengers at stations and the conditions of all those who work in the industry away from the public gaze.

The sectorization of the nationalized railway businesses from the 1980s onwards and the early years of the privatized railway businesses from 1994 targeted a number of initiatives to ensure that the building stock was considerably updated and put into a condition fit for the future. Much of this, at the major stations in particular, was made possible by related commercial development and, for instance, the extension of retail opportunities at stations. Although these changes may not have met the approval of all observers, they have been pivotal as has the influence of behind-the-scenes professionals, many of whom were architects, working to brief the many contractors and consultants involved. This process continues with the development of client-side design briefs, design reviews and design approvals.

It is inevitable that the different periods of history identified in these pages reflect different architectural styles and solutions but it may have been expected that the outputs of the private and public ownership periods, particularly in approaches to 'standardization' would be more distinct than is in fact the case. This is partly due to the continuation of regional or company structures from one period to the next and the fact that the offices and practices serving these regions had very strong individual characteristics. Centrally based resources concentrated on the less obviously regional work such as offices, hotels, centralized computer centres, hoverports and so on. What is clear now is that there are as many different solutions and approaches to solutions as there are contractors and design consultants employed at any one time, a situation that perhaps reflects the earlier days of the railways more than realized, despite the underlying technical standards that would be common across building types.

The need for a client to articulate what needs to be achieved in a building project and for those responsible for the design of the final product to meet these needs is still the key to a successful building. For some clients this means a direct and personal relationship with the designer even if this is sometimes fraught or fiery. The period of architectural development of the railway estate has seen this relationship vary many times as construction management and project management methodologies have changed, particularly since the advent of the twenty-first century. It is now possible that the architect can be unknown to the client, all interfaces being managed by the appointed contractor or project manager. In these circumstances, it is recognized that the commissioning company needs to carefully articulate its design aspirations – if it has any – via the development of design standards or guidance to be adopted by all those involved in the production of a building.

A particular requirement of all design teams engaged in this field is an understanding of the unique railway operational requirements in respect of safety, accessibility and inclusivity, capacity, sustainability and railway asset management and maintenance. These attributes form the backbone of design drivers for the commissioned resource and design review on behalf of the client groups, which also has to reflect all the other cornerstones of good design, particularly in the civic context.

In reviewing the architectural output of the railway companies across all eras it should perhaps be understood that each successive era had to work with the outputs of the former era and that there is a limited opportunity for entirely new expression until the advent of new railway lines such as HS1, HS2 and Crossrail.

The range of buildings and structures requiring the services of architecturally skilled in-house staff or appointed consultants remains high. With the more recent advent of new lines and services, the demand is actually growing.

As with much other public architecture, railway architecture reflects so many contemporary social and cultural values in addition to its core performance and functional values. Not only that but it attracts attention from observers worldwide, and is viewed with equal shares of admiration, exasperation and affection by users and local communities alike.

The variety and type of extant railway buildings, particularly stations, has never been greater with all ages and styles represented. Where these have statutory protection they should remain in a condition where they can be observed, experienced or enjoyed by many future generations. Selecting and keeping the examples for discussion within this book down to a manageable level has presented an exhausting challenge as every decade of the railway network's history has presented fascinating dilemmas and building solutions. One of these challenges has been to ascribe the designs of a building to a particular designer or practice, knowing that in many cases the design has gone through development stages with different appointments for each stage. A concern expressed by many in the design professions is that this can impact on the architectural quality of the final project, particularly if there is no client vision for what needs to be achieved.

Devising development and design solutions that meet all stakeholder requirements and expectations in this environment and context is one of the key challenges for anyone involved in the continual development of the rail network. Doing this within an architectural inheritance as historically rich and rewarding as our railway system should be seen as a challenge and a privilege.

Bibliography

The history of all aspects of the railway is comprehensively covered by many authors working as academics, professional authors or amateur enthusiasts. In writing this book we acknowledge all those who over many years have contributed to the body of knowledge that has, and still does, inform and enlighten all those who have an interest in railway architecture.

The range of information available is extensive and in producing this book we have used much of our own personal knowledge collected over many years of involvement with the world of railway architecture. Within this time, many works have become regarded as standard references and we have, as a matter of course, ensured that, where possible, our text takes account of these in the interests of consistency.

The references that have been of immense help in producing this book are, amongst others, listed below.

Anderson, V.R. and Fox, G.K., *A Pictorial Record of L.M.S. Architecture* (Oxford Publishing Company, 1981)

Biddle, G., *Britain's Historic Railway Buildings* (Ian Allan, 2003 & 2011)

Binney, M. and Pearce, D., *Railway Architecture* (Bloomsbury Books, 1979)

Binney, M. and Pearce, D. (eds), *Off the Rails: Saving Railway Architecture* (SAVE Britain's Heritage, 1977)

Bonavia, M.R., *Historic Railway Sites in Britain* (Robert Hale Ltd, 1987)

Buck, G., *A Pictorial Survey of Railway Stations* (Oxford Publishing Company, 1992)

Butt, R.V.J., *The Directory of Railway Stations* (Patrick Stephens Ltd, 1995)

Carter, O., *British Railway Hotels, 1838–1983* (Silver Link Publishing, 1990)

Cousins, J., *British Rail Design* (Danish Design Council, 1986)

Fawcett, W., T*he North Eastern Railway's Two Palaces of Business* (Friends of NRM, 2006)

HMSO, *The Reshaping of British Railways Part 1 and Part 2* (Harper Collins, 2013 (reprint of HMSO))

Houghton, F.W. and Hubert Foster, W., *The Story of the Settle–Carlisle Line* (Arch Publications, 1948)

Middleton, J. and Wikeley, N., *Railway Stations: Southern Region* (Peco Publications, 1971)

Russell, J., *Great Western Horse Power* (Oxford Publishing Company, 1995)

Thomas, R.G., *London's First Railway – The London & Greenwich* (B.T. Batsford Ltd, 1972 & 1986)

Vaughan, A., *Great Western Railway Architecture* (Oxford Publishing Company, 1977)

Woodfin, R.J., *The Cornwall Railway* (Bredford Barton, 1972)

A Glance Forward and a Look Back: BR brochure

The Development of the Central Station Site into the G-Mex Centre: Compiled by Nina Spooner, Central

Aspects of Railway Architecture: City of Bristol Planning and BR

British Rail Architecture, Design and Environment BRB, 1989

The New Euston Station 1968 (Opening Brochure): BR 35028/3

Further reading

There are many books that focus on rail operations and trains in particular and many of these have very helpful and informative images of railway buildings, particularly stations and signal boxes. However, it would not be possible to list all these. For this reason, the selection of suggested further reading highlights only those that relate specifically to the planning and architecture of such buildings or the people responsible for designing and building them.

Allen, D. and Woolstenholmes, J., *A Pictorial Survey of Railway Signalling* (Oxford Publishing Company, 1991)

Barman, C., *An Introduction to Railway Architecture* (Art and Technics Ltd, 1950)

Bennett, P., *The Architecture and Infrastructure of Britain's Railways: Northern England and Scotland* (Amberley, 2018)

Biddle, G., *The Railway Surveyors* (Ian Allan, 1990)

Bryan, T., *Railway Stations* (Amberley, 2017)

Burman, P. and Stratton, M. (eds), *Conserving the Railway Heritage* (E & FN SPON, 1997)

Fawcett, B., *Railway Architecture* (Shire, 2015)

Hickman, S. and Minnis, J, *The Railway Goods Shed and Warehouse in England* (Historic England, 2016)

Jenkins, S., *Britain's 100 Best Railway Stations* (Viking, 2017)

Lawrence, D., *British Rail Architecture 1948–97* (Crecy, 2018)

Meeks, C.L.V, *The Railroad Station* (Castle Books, 1978)

Minnis, J., *Britain's Lost Railways* (Aurum Press, 2011)

Parissien, S., *The English Railway Station* (English Heritage, 2014)

York, T., *Britain's Railway Architecture and Heritage* (Countryside Books, 2014)

York, T., *Victorian Railway Stations* (Countryside Books, 2015)

Building-specific Titles

Brindle, S., *Paddington Station – Its History and Architecture* (2nd edition) (English Heritage, 2013)

Derbyshire, N., *Liverpool Street: A Station for the Twenty-First Century* (Granta Editions, 1991)

Dyke, A., Durant, S., Gambrill, B. et al, *The Transformation of St Pancras International* (Laurence King, 2008)

Merrick, J., *Transforming King's Cross* (Merrell, 2012)

Thorne, R. and Simmons, J., *St Pancras Station* (Historical Publications, 2012)